NO ONE IS TOO OLD
TO LEARN

NO ONE IS TOO OLD TO LEARN

✦

Neuroandragogy: A Theoretical Perspective on Adult Brain Functions and Adult Learning

Clive A. Wilson

iUniverse, Inc.
New York Lincoln Shanghai

NO ONE IS TOO OLD TO LEARN
Neuroandragogy: A Theoretical Perspective on Adult Brain Functions and Adult Learning

iUniverse books may be ordered through booksellers or by contacting:

iUniverse
2021 Pine Lake Road, Suite 100
Lincoln, NE 68512
www.iuniverse.com
1-800-Authors (1-800-288-4677)

ISBN-13: 978-0-595-38766-3 (pbk)
ISBN-13: 978-0-595-83148-7 (ebk)
ISBN-10: 0-595-38766-7 (pbk)
ISBN-10: 0-595-83148-6 (ebk)

Printed in the United States of America

Contents

List of Illustrations

List of Tables

FOREWORD

The term "Andragogy" was coined and first appeared in published form in 1833 by German School Teacher, Alexander Kapp in his book entitled *Platon's Erzie hungslehre* (Plato's Educational Ideas)(See Apendix). He intended andragogy to be the education adults experienced which included and combined the education of inner, subjective personality ('character') and outer, objective competencies. Kapp also promoted andragogy as learning that takes place beyond self-reflection and life experience and, that it is more than just teaching adults (photo-copies of early German works can be found in the appendix).

Since Kapp's time andragogy as a term, as a theory, as a subject and as a science has been studied widely and has gained international recognition, developing deep roots in spite of repeated philosophical and ideological transformation. Historically speaking, when adult education became a field of theorizing in Germany in the 1920's, the term andragogy was not in use and had not been for more than 85 years. A reintroduction of the term brought a change to the direction of educational theory and practice. Andragogy then became the description of sets of explicit reflections, related to the why, what for, and how of teaching adults. With the passing years, andragogy was declared in different ways, such as the true method by which adults keep themselves intelligent about the modern world, and representing the learning process in which theory and practice become one.

With new insights in adult learning habits, scientific research, as well as modern approaches to theory and practice, a new foundation for Andragogy began to emerge. By the 1980's andragogy began to take on a professional appearance and soon became recognized by some researchers as a fairly independent scientific discipline, and was established as a subject of study. Through the years andragogy's growth has resulted from changes and also additions of empirical research to its scientific foundation.

Clive Wilson's original edition of *No One Is Too Old To Learn: Neuroandragogy: A Theoretical Perspective On Adult Brain Functions And Adult Learning,* represents such an addition, and is a landmark in the presentation of a scientific foundation for research in adult learning and its roots in and relationship to the adult human brain. This is the only book I know that delivers such in-depth information and research about the scientific foundation of how adults learn. In this book, Clive has focused purposefully on the adult brain, its cognitive functions, its graduation, and its relationship to the education and learning process of the adult. This book is an important contribution to our literature as well as a valuable resource for those individuals who wish to contribute to andragogy as a scientific discipline of study.

John A. Henschke
St. Louis, Missouri

PREFACE

New discoveries about the brain have caused great excitement and noticeable changes in disciplines that have applied the new findings. Many of the old beliefs have now been proven to be "myths", and new research results are forcing us to think differently about our brain and how it works. Some of the findings are so revolutionary that scientists have gained new hope regarding recovery of brain dementia and new ideas have developed relating to human learning and memory. This book is written with the hope that it will bring the same excitement and energy, experienced in other fields, to the discipline of andragogy by exploring the new research in conjunction with adult learning and aging.

To date, the main contribution to the development of the field has come from humanistic philosophy, developmental psychology, behavioral sciences and psychological measurements. Although these sciences have been helpful in forming principles and setting educational guidelines they have fallen short in explaining the true uniqueness of adult learning, and what really differentiates adult students from children. Conventional studies in education say very little about adult learning because most research and studies have put the emphasis on childhood learning and childhood development. This is also true regarding recent works in brain research and its application to education. The application to adult learning is limited when compared with the attention given to childhood education. This book seeks to address this neglect by turning to research that supplies information about the unique qualities of the aging brain and brain functions, dispelling myths and re-examining conventional wisdom which holds that learning cannot be achieved beyond a certain level of maturation.

I have chosen the neurosciences as a point of departure, focusing on its historical and current scientific development, documenting and applying fresh information to achieve a positive understanding, of adult learning and the aging process. This new model is a departure from research that promotes aging as decrepit, debilitating and depleting. This model embraces optimistic discoveries that reveal pictures of the aging brain's capacity to repair, maintain, and adapt. It celebrates the notion that there are ways to compensate for aging; that new growth and improvement is always a possibility, and experience and wisdom are gained through aging.

Although this book has gleaned heavily from the fields that study biological substrates of adult mental functions so as to make accurate applications and conclusions, it is not intended to be a text book for students of the biological sciences. Neither is this book written with the intent to add new knowledge to the field of neurology, but it may be of interest to those in this field who are intrigued with adult learning habits. In an effort to make this book interesting to a wider readership I have included many diagrams to help in the explanation of things biological. I have also synthesized facts from disciplines other than the neurosciences, but have not shied away from explaining learning at the cellular and synaptic level, which gives the book an academic appeal. This does not mean it cannot be understood by the lay person. It is my hope that students and teachers of andragogy, for whom this book is written, will gain interest in this new approach, and the book will be clear in its explanation that adults are never too old to learn: that the differences between the adult learner and the child begin with changes at the cognitive level.

While we may never know all there is to know about the human brain, most scientists will agree that there is adequate information now available to make informed decisions to effect change. This book is written to inform and educate, and I hope it does just that.

ACKNOWLEDGMENTS

My attainment authoring this book is first and foremost to the favor of Jesus Christ, Lord of my life. To him I give thanks for His boundless grace and mercy throughout this endeavor.

I would like to dedicate this work in memory of the late Dr. Bryon McKissack, former professor of Adult Education at Oral Roberts University of which I am a graduate. He always encouraged his students to write and publish. Thanks to Dr. Timothy Norton, also of Oral Roberts University, who believed in my ability to accomplish this great task and aided extensively in the editing of the manuscript. Special thanks to Dr. Ron Newsom of the University of North Texas, who introduced me to the studies of andragogy and always held an interest in my accomplishments. Thanks to Dr. John Henschke of Missouri State University, St. Louis, I could not have completed this work without his keen interest and knowledgeable input. A special thanks for his willingness to write the Foreword. Thanks to Dr. Rodney Myers, Neurologist, and Dr. Dale Jeffus, Psychologist, both associated with Hillcrest Medical Center in Tulsa, Oklahoma.

To Irene and Larry, who are responsible for the typing of the book many times over, thanks for their patience; John Mauldin for editing the first manuscript and to my dear friend Elise who did the final reading. To Dee Harris, for her skilled art work of each illustration, including the cover of the book. Thanks to the staff at Borders Book Store in Tulsa, Oklahoma, and Victor, New York, for taking care of me while I wrote. A special thanks to my friends in Indiana, Peggy and Keith, for letting me use their home by Skinner Lake to do research for this book. Thanks to Danielle Walters and Anita Pudusseri of New York, for their invaluable input.

To my many friends who encouraged me, always asking, "how is the book coming?" Thanks for pushing me along.

Finally, thanks to a lovely family. My wife Dureen has been my personal coach and editor; my son Gareth has shown remarkable interest in my work, and my daughter Nathlie promoted the book even before the completion of the first manuscript.

1

INTRODUCTION

Who said "you can't teach old dogs new tricks"? Those who have spent a lifetime working with adult learners will certainly disagree. This conventional wisdom has been challenged by years of successful empirical research in the learning sciences.

This old adage is a dismantled myth which revealed the prejudice in favor of childhood education, unwittingly aided mainly by the field of psychology and its sub-field psychometrics. This has left adult education under studied, under researched and under funded (Jeffus 2003).

Mainstream researchers in the field of adult learning are now agreeing that, No One Is Too Old to Learn. There is no set time for learning to occur, meaning, adults can learn beyond a certain level of maturation with the ability to reverse decline in intellectual functions through training and education. This was not always a popular view. The tradition of adult learning has always been filled with negatives, and is now beginning to change because of new findings in brain research. The work of early psychologists, and philosophers, produced empirical and theoretical studies that formed a scientific foundation for adult learning concerns. This knowledge in turn was incorporated in the existing body of knowledge which controls adult education. Today, however this body of knowledge is being critiqued by those concerned with new developments in brain research and its applications to learning and education. Those concerned also support a progressive education reform. Contemporary educators are seeking new ground and are slowly moving away from many of the traditional practices and theories long held in education.

With new developments in the neurosciences and related fields, the way is now being paved for a paradigm shift from old schools of thought to more recent research. There is now a new preference for hard scientific data. Progressive educators are seeking a link with biological sciences so as to gain a scientific understanding of the brain. This is the concern of this book, the development of a science that will improve on the understanding of why we are never too old to learn, how learning occurs even into our late years, and what really differentiates adult learners from children.

WHAT IS NEUROANDRAGOGY?

Neuroandragogy examines the evolution of neuroscience and Andragogy. It investigates the rigorous research of scholars in brain studies, the scientific investigation of adult learning and the evaluation of adult intelligence. Facts gathered from this effort are used to address problems pertaining to learning in conjunction with aging. This theory may further be defined as an anatomical and physiological study of the adult brain and its cognitive functions through its developmental process, indicating the systems of the brain that participate in intelligence, memory, recall and learning in general.

The study of neuroandragogy is new and is unique because it aims to investigate specifically the role the brain plays in the mental activity of adult learning. It also aims to focus on problems of learning and the aging brain, as are highlighted by research and practice. Most concerns in the field have stemmed from the notion that adults do not possess the ability to learn into old age. As a result, this book focuses on the functions of the adult brain, making a case for life long learning. The effect of experience on the brain is also examined along with other concerns, such as; will our brain always be able to modify itself throughout adulthood, or will we experience a drastic decline in brain plasticity as we age? Does memory and recall decline through life affecting new learning? If so, is there a way to stop this decline? Also, are we to expect decline in intelligence as we get older? Are there ways to offset intelligence decline?

There is new research included in this book that will aid in addressing these concerns. The book also examines exciting new studies regarding brain cell development late in life, and the notion of a positive correlation between higher education and the absence of the manifestation of Alzheimer's disease.

This book links neuroscience with andragogy forming a foundational base for research and theory. From the studies in neuroscience we gain information on the brain in an anatomical and physiological way, looking at the functions of neurons or nerve cells, synapses, axons, and neurotransmitters, as they relate to adult learning. From andragogy we gain a historical perspective on adult education practices, learning problems, learning theories and concepts on adult intelligence.

How This Book Is Designed

This book begins with the history and development of research in brain studies, analyzing the principal sources of the science that explains the changes in the adult brain. The brain functions are examined with close attention given to learning, plasticity, experience, intelligence, memory/recall, and psychometrics. All these areas are addressed in relationship to adult learning. Current research is analyzed for usefulness in adult education. The book then looks at the history and development of andragogy. A careful study is then done on the adult brain differences, making a case for adult learning differences. New theoretical perspectives are then introduced with some practical suggestions for educators. The final chapter lays out the tenets of this new theory.

This writing on neuroandragogy is not intended to be conclusive, but rather just the beginning to a turn in the road of adult learning and education. It is intended to encourage adult learning and research by students and scholars alike.

In this book I have intentionally minimized my discussion on methodology and techniques and placed the emphasis on theory so that a new foundation may be laid for upcoming research and practice in adult learning and education.

2

THE DEVELOPMENT OF BRAIN RESEARCH

The general fields that investigate brain functions, brain growth, perception, memory, learning and recall, can be traced back to the Egyptians of 1300 B.C. The first known recorded mention of the brain occurs in a surgical papyrus written about 1700 B.C. which is believed to be a copy of a much older surgical treatise dating back to 1300 B.C. (Gross, 1998; Finger, 2000). Finger theorizes that this period was the beginning of neuroscience. Greek rule of ancient Egypt 332 B.C. saw the acclamation of Imhotep's fame as a physician and his distinction as a god after his death. The Greeks joined the Egyptians in worshiping Imhotep. Influenced by Egyptian medicine, the Greeks researched the brain. Hippocrates (460–377 B.C.) and later Galen (A.D. 130–200), both of whom were Greek physicians, are recorded as having developed theories regarding the function of the brain. Hippocrates specifically concerned himself with theories of personality and its three types of bodily fluids, which he called humors. Galen researched the brains of pigs in order to ascertain the nature of substance of the brain, which he called the soul of the brain (Gross, 1998; Restak, 2000).

Historical and medical records lack information relating to brain research for the next one thousand two hundred years. The next mention of brain research was in the works of Leonardo da Vinci (1452–1519). While da Vinci researched brain tissue, his contemporary, Andreas Kesalius, experimented on the brains of executed criminals to prove a central system in the mind. Both men sought to prove the centrality of brain function. Two centuries later Reni Descartes (1596–1650) and Thomas Willis, both French scientists, developed the theory of dualism, agreeing with earlier theorists, which taught that the brain and mind are separate. His conclusion resulted from the observation of collapsing brains and their rapid deterioration after dissection. He proposed that in the living brain the ventricles served as receptacles for a fluid believed to be the means of nervous transmission (Restak, 2000; Finger, 2000). Although Thomas Willis also supported the theory of dualism, it was of a different kind. He believed the brain to be divided into separate regions: mental, or memory, will or imagination (Restak, 2000).

One hundred years after Descartes and Willis, German physician Franz Gall (1758–1828) favored localization of the brain. As a result, he established the science of phrenology (the evaluation of personality by irregularities in the skull, see Fig 1). Gall is considered responsible "for the ideas we now hold on the relations which the constituent parts of the nervous system bear to one another" (Gregory, 1998, p. 282). He was the first scientist to distinguish clearly the white matter of the brain which consists of fibers responsible for the connection of neurons, and the gray matter which forms the cortex of the brain, composed of brain cells or neurons (Gregory, 1998; Gross, 1998).

Opposition to Gall's hypotheses came from Jean Marie Fiqurens, a nineteenth-century French physiologist. He preferred the alternative theory of a divided brain carrying out specialized functions also known as holism (Restak, 2000).

Italian scientist Luigi Galvani (1737–1798) was the first to experiment with the view that the nerves and muscles work by generating electricity. Emil Heinrich Du Bois-Reymond (1818–1896), a German biologist, followed the work of Galvani. Du Boise-Reymond's work was considered fundamentally important. He experimented with the field of electrical discharge and discovered electrical activity and chemical changes in the nerves and muscles. He is regarded as the first scientist to attempt an explanation of all functions of the brain, relating it to chemical and physical activity (Bloom & Lazerson, 1988; Gregory, 1998).

By the nineteenth century many medical investigators provided a wave of understanding about the brain. Much of the discoveries were accomplished by observation and experimentation. German physiologist Friedrich Galtz (1824–1902), Edward Hitzig (1838–1907) and his co-worker Gustav Fritsch all worked on experiments related to the cortical motor area of the brain. Through their experiments, with the removal of large amounts of the cerebral cortex of the brains of animals, they were able to locate the exact area of motor cortex. Hitzig's and Fritsch's discovery of the cortical motor area has been regarded as the most significant laboratory discovery in brain research (Bloom & Lazerson, 1988; Finger, 2000).

The twentieth century found researchers concerned with the functions of the brain cells performing the work of the brain. The effort of scientists was now to determine "whether the process of transmission between neurons was electrical or

The science of phrenology held that one's personality can be evaluated by the irregularites in the skull. This theory was introduced by Franz Gall, a German physician in the 18th century.

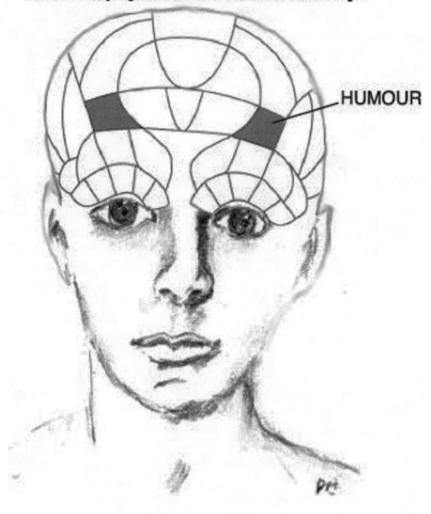

HUMOUR

Figure 1 Franz Gall's Phrenology

chemical" (Bloom & Lazerson, 1988, p. 18). Otto Loewi (1873–1961), a German biologist, and English pharmacologist, Sir Henry Dale (1875–1961) made this chemical-transmission hypothesis clear through their experiments, which brought new ways of thinking about the communications of neurons. Their studies concluded that axon endings liberate chemicals to stimulate or inhibit other cells (Bloom & Lazerson, 1988; Finger, 2000).

An interest in brain research soon caught on in the U.S. as seen in the work of John Warren (1778–1856), John Bell (1796–1872) and Charles Caldwell (1772–1853) who carefully examined neuroscience and, in particular, the theory of phrenology, as illustrated in Fig. 2. The death of German physiologist Friedrich Galtz in 1902, a then strong promoter of the theory in America, caused the dwindling of the theory making room for other studies in the neurosciences (Finger, 1994). Studies of brain compartmentalization by Robert Bartholow (1831–1904) and Ivory Franz (1874–1933) soon led to the investigation of the work being done in Germany and England regarding neurons and axons. Roger Sperry (1913–1994) led this research in America and was later recognized as an outstanding neurobiologist. Some of his work led to exploring the growth of axons in their proper places and their direction to their targets by chemical attractions. Sperry's interest included the processing of information between the hemispheres of the brain and with the help of his student, Ronald Myers (1950), he performed split brain experiments. Results of these experiments led Sperry to conclude consciousness must be a higher property of the brain with the ability to modify the other processes (Finger, 2000).

Brain-based knowledge, as it is known today, has been acquired over the past 200 years (Restak, 2000). However, it appears to be the work of the 1950's to 1980's that is of real importance, since it is in this period that imaging technology began to be used as a tool to understand the brain.

NEW FIELDS OF STUDY

Neuroscience.

Neuroscience as a separate field of study began in this new era and is derived in part from the merging of three other disciplines: neuroanatomy, neurophysiology, and neurochemistry. These fields began to be integrated in the early 1950's with the introduction of two new study techniques, electron microscopy (used in neuroanatomy), and intracellular electrical recording (used in neurophysiology) (Dowling, 1992).

The theory of phrenology became a serious study in America in the late 18th century, headed by three medical doctors, John Warren, John Bell and Charles Caldwell.

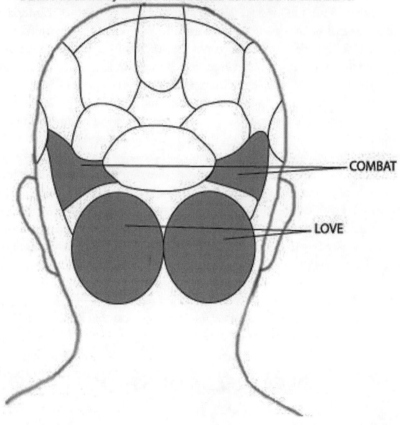

Figure 2 U.S. medical doctors also believed in phrenology

These and other advanced technologies permit the study of brain biology, brain chemistry, and brain physiology by viewing the brain in cross-sectional pictures, catching sections of specific points in specific areas of the brain, and by providing real-time images of blood flow patterns that show the active parts of the brain (Howard, 2000).

With the integration of neurochemistry, anatomy and physiology, the term neuroscience became recognized, and is now generally used for the study of the brain. In laboratories today neuroscientists are joined by computer scientists, psychologists, and molecular biologists seeking answers to brain function (Dowling, 1992). The development of interdisciplinary work in this field has given rise to new terms, one of which is cognitive neuroscience.

Cognitive neuroscience.

Advances in brain research in the 1980's gave birth to the interdisciplinary work of cognitive neuroscience. For more than two hundred years psychology was developed independently from neurological studies: while psychology concerned itself with the studying of the mind and consciousness, studies of the nervous system concentrated specifically on the functions of the brain. Bruer (1999) explains the differences. Psychology, he says, studies our mental software and neuroscience our neural hardware. He defines cognitive neuroscience as a new field of about fifteen years, focusing upon the brain structure supports of mental functions.

This new field has presented a convergence of data from research in neuroscience, psychology, cognitive psychology, neuropsychology, and neurophysiology in an attempt to understand the brain's role in cognitive functions. Details about the measurement of human brain activity, information coding, neural mechanisms of memory, working memory, consciousness, learning, experience and recall, form a valuable body of information, describing intellectual development. Much of the research findings are a result of the advent of non-invasive imaging technologies. The most recent of these being Position Emission Topography (PET), and Functional Magnetic Resonance Imaging (FMRI). These technologies have been used to directly observe the human brain (Branford, Brown & Cocking, 1999; Rugg, 1997, see figures 3 & 4).

Cognitive neuroscience has also produced insights into the development of the brain, mainly the cerebral cortex and its relation to thinking and learning.

Functional magnetic resonance imaging (FMRI) sometimes called MRI or NMR--nuclear magnetic resonance imaging work with a combination of atomic particles (placed in the body by magnetism and radio waves.)

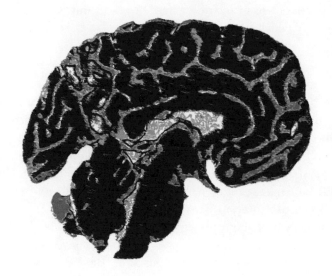

Figure 3 Functional Magnetic Resonance Imaging

Position Emission Topography (PET) is very similar to fMRI but does not produce the same fine resolution as the fMRI, and requires an injection of radioactive marker in the bloodstream.

Figure 4 Position Emission Topography

Such insights carry great implications for educational practice and policy (Fischer & Rosi, 1998). Current researchers are concerning themselves even more with changes the brain is able to make through growth cycles. This cyclical property is said to explain the remarkable human capacity for plasticity (1998). Cognitive neuroscience is also seeking to make the right connection between plasticity and the duration of the mental capacities of the aging. Early studies indicated a rapid decline in intellectual capacity with age, attributing this to the loss of brain function. Key findings now hold that intelligence does decline with chronological age, but not as rapidly as first believed. Now it is said that the decrease does not normally begin until relatively late in life (Shaie as cited in Tennant & Pogson, 1995).

With the replacement of old research by the new, some educators are beginning to show interest in the current information regarding the brain. As knowledge of brain plasticity and the duration of intelligence goes through changes, educators must also prepare themselves to work with the differences in the understanding of the connection between the development of the brain and learning to achieve better results (Diamond, 1988; Tennant & Pogson, 1995).

Cognitive neuroscience also links observations about cognitive behavior with the physical processes that support such behavior. This study finds important the area of the brain that controls basic sensory motor functions; the area that controls emotions, memory and biorhythms; and the area that controls cognition, reasoning, language and intelligence. Cognitive neuroscientists reject the notion of comparing the brain to a computer because the structure of the brain's neuron connections are loose, flexible, webbed and redundant. The brain does not function like a linear or parallel-processing machine, it is considered a self-organizing system. What is more, cognitive neuroscientists conclude that the brain changes with use throughout its lifetime. Memory develops by certain patterns of mental connections which alter the physical structure of the brain. Each connection makes it easier to create another the next time. Proponents of cognitive neuroscience advocate continued learning throughout adulthood, and intellectual incline (On Purpose Associates, 2001).

More importantly studies in neuroscience and cognitive neuroscience provide for neuroandragogy a clear understanding of the functions of the adult brain. The documentation of new research in these fields provides a plethora of information on the brain, its development and changes into later life. The following chapter investigates the general knowledge of the brain and special areas of interest that relate specifically to the concerns of this book.

3

WHAT WE KNOW ABOUT THE HUMAN BRAIN

While the fields of neuroscience and cognitive neuroscience are concerned with the intricate details of the brain, neuroandragogy seeks mainly to probe the basic brain functions and in particularly those that address the problems of learning and memory as they concern adults. It is therefore most fitting to begin with an understanding of the most prominent parts of the human brain, brain cells and areas of special interest.

THE THREE MOST PROMINENT PARTS OF THE HUMAN BRAIN

The human brain is considered the most complex thing in the universe. No one knows everything there is to know about the brain. However there seems to be enough information to give us a start in understanding the most important organ in the body, as well as the most used. The brain takes in information around us, coordinates the body's movements and processes our thoughts. This magnificent organ known as the brain has been divided into three parts for a better understanding.

Cerebrum.

This is the largest section of the brain which has three distinct areas, the sensory, the motor, and the association areas. The sensory areas are responsible for incoming signals from taste, smell, touch, sight, and hearing. All these sensations provide the brain with information. The motor areas are responsible for voluntary movement, and the association area is the link to the sensory and motor areas responsible for; thought, learning, language, memory, judgment and personality. The cerebrum is the center of intellect, memory, consciousness, language and sensation. It is divided into right and left hemispheres which have lobes: the frontal lobe is found at the front of the brain; the parietal lobe is at the top of the brain; the temporal lobes is at the sides of the brain; and the occipital is found at the back of the brain. Most of us are acquainted with the concept of the brain being covered with gray matter, this is also known as the cerebral cortex which is arranged into folds or layers that increase the surface area. Some people refer to this area as the thinking area or the thinking brain. Here is where much of our memory is stored. This region of the brain contains the motor, sensory, and association cortex. Beneath the gray matter is the white matter which has millions of cells each connected to the other. These cells are also known as myelinated axons or neurons that connect various regions of the brain. These axons are arranged into various bundles or tracts. These cells are believed to be responsible for the brain's communication (Solomon, et. al., 1999, and Newquist, 2004) The heavily folded surface is called the gyri or singular gyrus, and the deep grooves are called the sulci or singular, sulcus. The deepest grooves are called fissures, and are responsible for dividing the right and left hemisphere, as well as the four main functional areas named earlier (Walker, 2002). Next in size and importance is the cerebellum.

Cerebellum.

The cerebellum is situated beneath the cerebrum. The term itself means "little cerebrum" and is also covered by the cortex. It is divided into two hemispheres and is as small as a golf ball and looks like a cauliflower. This region of the brain is responsible for the coordination of all our motions and movements. Although smaller than the cerebrum, this area of the brain has more nerve cells. While the cerebellum cannot tell how to ride a bike it will coordinate the bike riding adventure. It will do the coordinating better than the cerebrum could describe the act of riding. Some people resort to showing instead of telling, this is the cerebellum at work (Newquist, 2004). If this region of the brain is injured, it affects the performance of voluntary movements, which then become clumsy (Solomon, et. al., 1999). The third prominent part is the brain stem.

Brain stem.

Although the smallest of all three regions, the brain stem is responsible for the tremendous job of carrying all messages from the brain to the body and back. It is responsible for the actions of living that we give very little thought to, pertaining to staying alive: such as breathing, blinking, heart rate, blood pressure, swallowing, coughing, body temperature, appetite, fat metabolism, etc. The brain stem contains the larger of the brain nerves known as the cranial nerves. These nerves control all the movements in the head. The brain stem is also divided in several parts; the medulla, the pons, the midbrain, the thalamus, and the hypothalamus. Each of these structures perform a specific function in relaying messages from body to brain and back (Newquist, 2004, and Solomon, et. al., 1999). All messages are relayed by brain cells.

There are one hundred trillion neurons or cells in the brain. The brain has ten types of command cells composed of neurons performing the basic command functions. Some of these are lost during the normal aging process. People who develop neurodegenerative disorders such as Alzheimer's disease or Parkinson's disease will lose them more rapidly. In the nucleus of these cells is the DNA (deoxyribonucleic acid), the source of our genetic code; they also contain mitochondria, which are the power providers of the cell energizing it to do its work of metabolism. The nucleus of the cell contains machinery that makes enzymes, proteins, neurotransmitters, all of which create the chemical messengers permitting nerve cells to communicate with each other, maintaining the cell's energy levels and eliminating waste products. These nerve cell bodies are surrounded by smaller, highly branched projections known as dendrites that permit neurons to inter-communicate over short distances and receive messages simultaneously (Andreasen, 2001).

The cerebral cortex or the bark of the brain is covered with nerve cell bodies which are highly concentrated on the surface giving it an appearance of being covered with bark. There are small concentrations of groups of nerve cells also deep inside the brain which are called subcortical regions or regions below the cortex. The brain's neurons are connected to one another for the purpose of sending messages back and forth to each other for relatively long distances. This connection is achieved by the projection of long arms from the neuron that look like wires. These are called axons. These axons are covered with fatty insulation known as myelin (See Fig. 5). The thickness of the myelin depends on cell function.

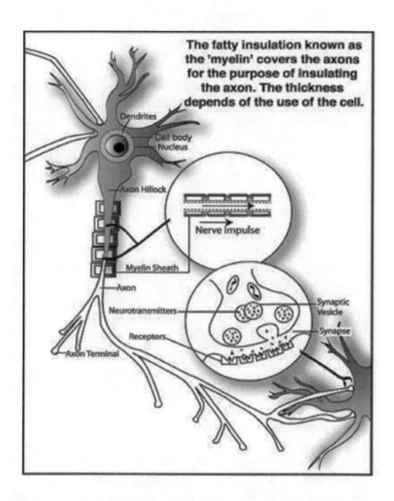

Figure 5 The fatty insulation is called Myelin

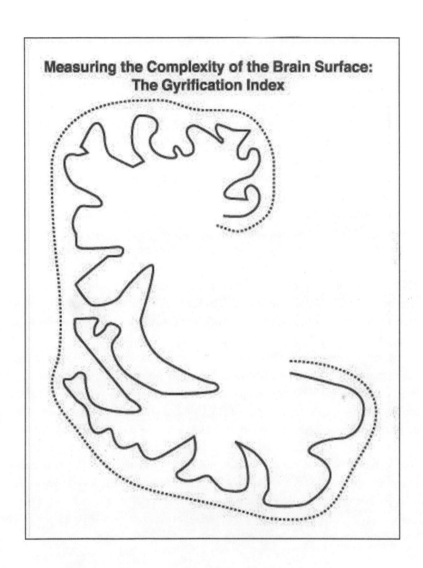

Figure 6 The Gyrification Index (GI)

Cells with little insulation send information faster than those heavily insulated. Most brain illnesses strike at the command center or the cell body. There are some that work their destruction on the white brain matter. These illnesses are called de-MYELIN-ating diseases, which include multiple sclerosis (MS) and amyotrophic lateral sclerosis (ALS or Lou Gehrig's Disease). These white matter diseases effectively interrupt the communication between nerve cells by cutting the neuron's wire. The brain is bathed by the cerebrospinal fluid (CFS) which contains nutrients and byproducts of brain activity. The regions containing CSF are known as ventricles. The monitoring of the amount of CSF present inside or on the surface of the brain is the method used to determine brain injury or degeneration. An increase in CSF on the brain or the growth of ventricles has been a clue used by doctors that brain tissue has decreased, indicating that something has probably gone wrong, since the increase of CSF replaces the missing brain tissue (Andreasen, 2001). In the same way the brain can be observed for defects it can also be measured for growth.

Andreasen records that the crumpled brain is a sign of brain growth (crumpling to fit the size of the skull). German neuroscientist, Karl Zilles, developed a method by which to measure the crumpling of the brain known as gyrification index or GI (See Fig. 6). This measuring method has proved helpful in understanding neurodevelopment and indicates slow development in human brains. Development scarcely begins at the time of birth, continues through infancy and adolescence to become fully developed in the early to mid-twenties. The human brain is essentially smooth until around the sixth month of fetal life with a GI of around 1.06. Comparatively a GI of 1.0 means the brain is totally smooth. It is at this period in human life that the major sulci and gyri begin to form and the complexity of the connections between nerve cells increase in the cerebral cortex. By birth the brain has a GI of around 1.15. The newborn baby is helpless and will need an adult's help for most of its early years. The GI changes and increases as the human brain mature, finally reaching normal adult level in the early twenties. The behavior of adolescents and their steady changes from impulsive response to social responsibilities are signs of brain development; the GI is increasing.

AREAS OF SPECIAL INTEREST

Neurophysiology and learning.

Thompson (1985) rightly states that if any one capability sets humans apart from animals it has to be learning and memory. He adds language, knowledge, culture and attitudes all are a result of learning. How learning takes place is an important issue in neuroscience and of key interest to neuroandragogy. Neuroscientists believe that finding answers leading to the understanding of memory and learning will help with the understanding of brain function. The more we understand how neurons are altered biochemically by synaptic input the better we will understand the neurophysiological changes caused by learning.

Early theories of memory and learning pointed to the involvement of specific cellular mechanisms. Raymon y Cajal was one of the first learning theorists who proposed that learning is the result of a change in the synaptic function. This theory held that when a specific pathway in the brain experiences repeated activity the synapses are affected causing long-lasting or even permanent changes. A second theory was that neurons sprout new processes and make new synapses as learning is happening. By the 1920's a new theory surfaced out of Harvard University. Dr. Alexander Forbes proposed the reverberating circuit theory, which was based on observations of persistent activity in neurons and pathways after stimulation. This activity, according to Forbes, did not cause any functional changes in synapses or neurons, neither did it cause any anatomical modification in the neurons. This theory did not withstand the compelling evidence argued against it. Another theory out of Harvard came from Dr. Karl Lashley a psychologist in the 1930's. He argued that learning is not an action of the cells, this is known as the aggregate field theory. His premise was that learning is an act of many parts of the brain and that specific cellular connections are less important. For Lashley, circuits are not important. It is how much of the brain is available that is important. For awhile his work was accepted but most recent research is showing evidence in favor of discrete cellular mechanisms which underlie memory and learning (Dowling, 1992).

Current theories hold that learning depends on synaptic plasticity which involves complex biochemical processes, including actions of neurotransmitters and postsynaptic receptors (Solomon, et. al., 1999). Evidence for specific and unique cells and synapses relating to learning comes from research done on invertebrates. The marine snail known as *Aplysia* has been studied for this purpose. As a result of these studies the pendulum has swung back to early ideas that synaptic modification is responsible for memory and learning (Dowling, 1992). Studies done for more than 30 years on the *Aplysia* have also resulted in new conclusions regarding memory and learning. Several neural processes have been studied, but three in particular have helped in the understanding of memory and learning: (1) habituation, (2) sensitization, and (3) classical conditioning (Solomon, et. al, 1999).

Habituation is regarded as the decrease in response which occurs after repeated exposure to a harmless stimulus. This process helps animals to ignore constant stimuli. When there is repeated stimulation sensory neurons release less neurotransmitter thus the action potentials in the motor neurons are decreased. This "decrease in neurotransmitter was traced to inactivation of calcium channels in the presynaptic terminals. This leads to the reduction of the number of cal cium ions entering the presynaptic terminals in response to repeated action potentials"(Solomon, et, al. 1999, p.864). It should be noted here, the more calcium ions set free the more stimulation there is and consequently more neurotransmitters are released.

Sensitization on the other hand happens when there is an increased response after the experience of an unpleasant stimulus. In the process of sensitization the brain experiences more calcium entering the axon terminal and more neurotransmitters being released. "This," says Solomon, et. al., (1999), "stimulates a stronger response in the postsynaptic motor neuron. Thus, sensitization depends on an increase in neurotransmitter released by the sensory neuron" (p. 863). This encounter creates structural changes in the sensory neurons (Dowlin, 1992). The third area of learning is classical conditioning also known as associative learning. Classical conditioning occurs when both habituation and sensitization pathways interact.

Classical conditioning was accidentally discovered by Russian biologist Ivan Pavlov who's experiment with a dog proved: if two stimuli are paired closely in time, and one stimulus produces a response and the other none, eventually the animal will respond to the unconditioned stimulus, when it is presented alone. This response will be the same as the response given the conditioned stimulus (Dowling, 1999). Thompson (1983) describes this learning as the type that occurs mainly with animals and that it works best when it has adaptive consequences, such as obtaining food or avoiding injury. As a result of studies on Pavlov's dog and the sea snail (Aplysia), biologists have concluded that classical conditioning requires NMDA (N-methl-D-aspartate) receptors that are involved in LTP (long-term potentiation).

These findings have led to describing memory and learning as being dependent on synaptic plasticity which involves complex biochemical processes. This process depends on actions of neurotransmitters and postsynaptic receptors. Long-term potentiation has been determined as an important mechanism in the learning process. It is the strong stimulation of a presynaptic neuron that strengthens the synapses, it also strengthens weakly stimulated synapses that are activated at the same time (See Fig. 10). This strong stimulation also leads to depolarization of the postsynaptic neuron which in turn triggers LTP. Some studies have shown that NMDA receptors are important in animals, and when these are blocked LTP does not occur. Figure 10 shows an example of how LTP works in animals. A presynaptic neuron releases glutamates which are believed to combine with non-NMDA receptors. When the postsynaptic neuron is depolarized magnesium moves from the NMDA receptors in turn unblocking them. As the NMDA receptors open calcium moves into the cell. This inflow of calcium appears to be an important trigger for LTP (Solomon, et. al., 1999).

Researchers believe calcium ions act as second messenger initiating long-term changes. Calcium may stimulate release of a signal that moves backwards from the postsynaptic neuron and would signal the presynaptic neuron. This signal would in turn enhance neurotransmitter release by the presynaptic neuron which makes the relationship between the two neurons stronger. Studies on the neurophysiology of learning and memory is still very new and in the future there maybe other mechanisms for LTP that will be discovered (Solomon, et. al., 1999).

Neurodevelopment.

Brain growth has been of great interest to scientists and the study of the process is now known as "neurodevelopment". Andreasen (2001) describes the process as a miraculous one, beginning a few months after conception (See Fig. 7). After a sufficient number of germ cells or neurons accumulate in the middle of the brain they begin to travel to various areas of the brain so that nerve cells, axons and dendrites can make connections to themselves and to each other to send the correct messages to the right places, to be stored or thrown out, reflected upon or acted upon (See Fig. 8). This process is known as "neuronal migration", identified by Pasko Rakic of Yale University.

These nerve cells, known as glia or glue, will arrive in a new territory and create their own colony. They eventually form the cerebral cortex and the subcortical gray matter regions of the brain. Connections are made by the axons that are later sent out. These divide into two parts, the left hemisphere and the right hemisphere. Both hemispheres communicate with each other, as shown in Fig. 9, creating what is known as the corpus callosum or the firm body (2001).

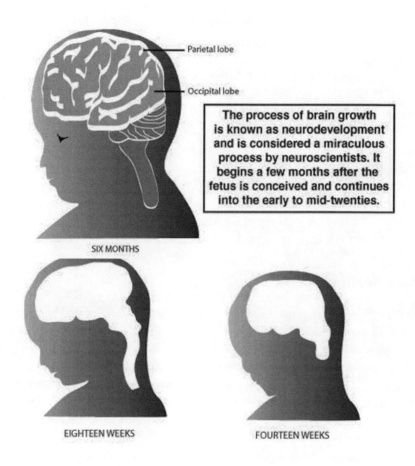

The process of brain growth is known as neurodevelopment and is considered a miraculous process by neuroscientists. It begins a few months after the fetus is conceived and continues into the early to mid-twenties.

Figure 7 Early neurodevelopment

A sufficient number of germ cells or neurons accumulate in the middle of the brain and travel to make connection with other nerve cells, axons and dendrites, a process in neurodevelopment called neuronal migration.

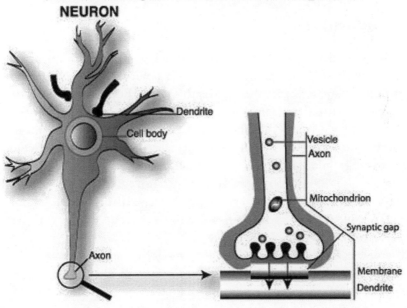

Figure 8 Neuronal Migration

The brain forms more cells than are needed, but as it matures the excess is steadily removed to form the correct balance of connections. This process is known as cell death and pruning. The communication points that permit the cells to talk to one another simultaneously are a process known as "synaptogenesis". There are several chemicals that travel across the synapses: dopamine; serotonin; norepinephrine; and glutamate. These chemicals interact with one another in order to create the right balance for rapid and efficient communication (Andreasen, 2001).

Neuroplasticity.

Neuroplasticity also called brain plasticity, is a very important concept. The notion of plasticity was made popular through the philosophies of both Emanuel Kant and his student, Johan Herbart in the eighteenth century. Both men insisted that only the young be offered the systematic method of education, one that occupied a particular time in life with a clear beginning and end. From this notion came the tradition of the "theory of plasticity" that "perpetuated the idea that adults could not learn, physically or intellectually, after a certain level of maturation" (Birren, 1988, p. 4; Savicevic, 1995). Robert Peers (1934), a British educator was one of the first persons to challenge the "theory of plasticity". He stated in his writing on the plastic years of the child that adults can learn too. He did not accept plasticity as a youthful experience only, neither does current research.

Neuroplasticity simply defined is, "the capacity of the brain to learn, remember, reorganize, and recover from damage" (Howard, 2000, p. 779). The concept emphasizes the dynamics of the brain, how it is able to change rapidly from moment to moment, responding to challenges from the outside environment. Some of these changes become permanently coded or stored for later use. Brain development is shaped by one's physical and psychological experiences, which may be quite arbitrary (Andreasen, 2001).

The best known theory of neuroplasticity is that of Canadian neuroscientist Donald Hebb, explained in his book, *The organization of behavior: a neuropsychological theory* (1949). Hebb argued that the brain's ability to change by learning new information happens because of changes that occur at the level of the nerve cells. Remodeling of the brain is achieved by the changing of connections at the level of the synapse. If many nerve cells receive a stimulus at the same time, they fire or produce action potential, and begin to share more and more synaptic connections. This explanation of plasticity became known as the Hebbian Plasticity. Andreasen says it is best stated in the motto "neurons that fire together wire together" (2001, p. 47).

It is now known that new wiring is achieved through a mechanism known as long-term potentiation (LTP). Andreasen described LTP as:

> The process by which the size of a neuronal response increases after stimulation. The increase in response ('potentiation') is relatively long lasting ('long-term'). This increase in neuronal response is one important mechanism by which long-term changes such as learning occur (2001, p. 48). The understanding of LTP gives the explanation as to how the brain changes at the cellular and molecular level when learning occurs. LTP is the process by which increase takes place in a neuronal response resulting after stimulation. The increase in response is called 'potentiation', which usually lasts for a while, thus known as 'long-term'. The neuronal response is important for long-term changes such as learning (Andreasen, 2001).

Meaningful education and experiences results in memory formation and storage. The higher the frequency of activity the stronger the synapses as explained earlier and displayed in figure 10. New connections at the level of the synapses made by neural activity are subject to the "use it or lose it" rule according to LeDoux (2002, p. 79). When new connections are made, only those that go on to be used survive. According to Hebbian plasticity, this occurrence is held accountable for the nature of learning and memory and other aspects of synaptic function, especially while synapses are in construction during development.

Hebb suggested that to increase efficiency of the new connections and maintain their connections, new growth needs to occur. At the time of Hebb's writings there was not much evidence of new growth, but since then activity-induced growth has been observed in many different circumstances. The manner in which activity encourages growth during early development is still under observation. In particular is a "class of post-synaptic receptors for the excitatory transmitter glutamate". This is a neurotransmitter that excites brain cells (Bloom, Beal & Kupfer 2003, p. 657; LeDoux, 2002, p. 81). These receptors are also known as NMDA (N-methyl-D-aspartate) which is "a glutamate essential for neuronal transmission and growth" (Howard, 2000, p. 779). Bert Sakman, one of the most noted contemporary German scientists who is involved in studies of memory functions regarding encoding and retrieval of information, found the NMDA receptor in the brain responsible for higher brain functions, which also include developmental changes and learning (Bass, 1994). These receptors have gained special interest because they are able to detect the match between activity in the presynaptic and postsynaptic neuron. The blocking of these receptors or any interference causes normal development to be disrupted (LeDoux, 2002).

The corpus callosum is generally thicker in females than in males and it carries more information between hemispheres. (Example is exaggerated.)

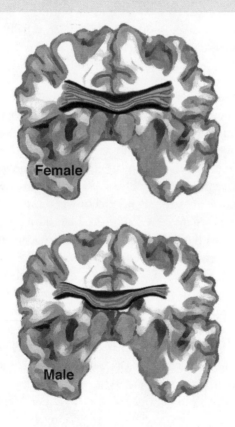

Figure 9 The corpus callosum

Meaningful education and experiences result in memory formation and storage. The higher the frequency of activity the stronger the synapses. This is known as Long Term Potentiation (LTP).

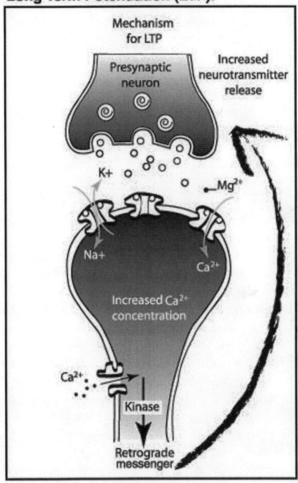

Figure 10 Long Term Potentiation (LTP)

Work done by David Hubel and Torsten Wiesel (Andreasen, 2001; LeDoux, 2002) in the 1960's gave additional insight to the understanding of plasticity from the perspective that experiences in the environment and use prevented synaptic demise.

Hubel and Wiesel, in their classic research, discovered that the environment can affect the development of the brain by way of the brain's vision center. If the vision center fails to receive guidance from the environment in the critical periods, nerve cells that develop sight will fail. A study was conducted on cats and monkeys early in their lives to examine later life effects. They found that when one eye is covered or removed early in life normal cellular alignment does not occur in the visual centers of the brain that can only receive input from the eye. In adulthood, when the eye is opened, few if any cells respond to visual stimulation. Hubel and Wiesel also found that the seeing eye adapted and took over the functions of the eye that could no longer see. This proved that there is a critical period for the vision center to be formed and that synaptic activity prevents cell death (Andreasen, 2001; LeDoux, 2002).

Neurogenesis.

Of great interest to contemporary neuroscientists is the finding of new cell growth in the matured brain. As early as the 1960's Mark Rosenzweig of the University of California at Berkeley discovered that rodents removed from their standard patterned laboratory conditions revealed proof of slightly heavier brains when placed in larger cages with more room and activity gadgets. Newly developed neurons were the cause for heavier brains, and the process became known as neurogenisis. This discovery, however, was rejected by conventional beliefs. Biology and physiology teach that there is no brain cell growth after birth, especially in human beings: that we are born with all the brain cells we will ever have, and as we age we lose some. Some scientists believe we begin losing cells at birth, others think we start at age twelve, concluding that the loss of a few million cells is affordable when compared with the total number with which we are born (Jensen, 1995; LeDoux, 2002).

However, these conventional views held by biologists and other scientists are presently being challenged by recent studies conducted by Erikson, McEwen, Gould, Gage, Ebner, and others who have demonstrated that neurons continue to be generated even in the human adult brain. The extent of new neurons and cell growth in the neocortex region of the brain is still left to be discovered (Camichael, 2000; LeDoux, 2001).

Studies conducted on older animals in the 1960's by Rosenzweig and later William Greenough of the University of Illinois described amazing brain improvement when living conditions were changed. By 1964 Altman suggested that the adult brain may also be experiencing the production of new nerve cells. This notion was quickly dismissed. By the 1980's biologists were overturning the old school of thought by finding a reservoir of stem cells that became fresh neurons in more than one part of the brain of adult birds, monkeys, and also humans. Fernando Nottebohm of the Rockefeller University took the lead in the 1980's with research on adult canaries and their song learning habits. New research with marmoset monkeys, conducted by Elizabeth Gould, Bruce McEwen and Ekerhard Fuchs in 1997, revealed neurogenisis occurring in the hippocampus. By 1999 Gould was reporting large numbers of new nerve cells in yet another part of the monkey brain, the neocortex. Gould strongly hinted that the same may even be happening to adults (Kempermann & Gage, 1999; Car michael, 2002).

Further research between 1996 and 1998 showed positive signs of nerve cell growth in the human brain, as displayed in Fig. 11. Peter Eriksson, of the Sahlgrenska University Hospital in Goteborg, Sweden, and Gage discovered that the bromodeox yuridine (BrdU) tracer, used in animals to detect new nerve cell growth in the brain, was being used in cancer patients. An investigation of brain tissue after their death displayed new neurons. These cancer patients ranged in age from 57 to 72. This growth was found in the hippocampus region of the brain. Cells known as granules in the dentate gyrus were outstanding (Kemper mann & Gage, 1999; Howard, 2000; Carmichael, 2002).

Neuroscientists are convinced there is still much more to learn regarding nerve cell growth. There are concerns, such as, how well will these new neurons work? Or do they work at all? Will they be able to send or receive messages in the right way? How or by what means will these new nerve cells be controlled? Which features of an enriched environment have the strongest effect on the new nerve cells? Finally, can this new growth repair the brain? These concerns will incorporate the practice of culturing human embryonic stem cells, which are highly versatile cells, capable of giving rise to virtually any cell type in the body. This is of great interest to medical doctors and also an ongoing ethical concern. Another problem to be faced is that of rejection. If these new cells are transplanted in damaged sites in an effort to replenish lost nerve cells, rejection by the body's immune system is possible. These and other studies on the human brain will require clever protocol. To move the study from rodents to people calls for noninvasive imaging techniques such as Functional Magnetic Resonance Imaging or Positron Emission Topography. If new nerve cells are stimulated or transplanted they must in turn be guided to perform correctly without interfering with normal brain function (Kempermann & Gage, 1999; Myers, 2002). These new findings have brought hope to brain scientists who must now revise virtually all ideas relating to human learning, memory and recovery of brain dementia (Carmichael, 2000; LeDoux, 2001).

It is believed that new brain cell growth in the matured brain is possible. The areas of great interest are the Neo-Cortex, the Olfactory Bulb and the Hippocampus.

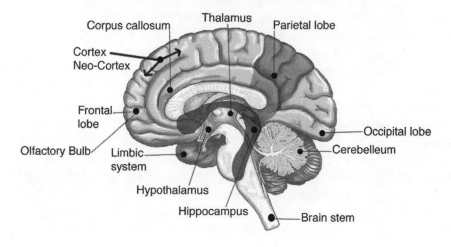

Figure 11 Areas of new brain cell growth in the human brain

4

BRAIN PLASTICITY AND ADULT LEARNING

Current research demonstrates growing interest in the changes the brain is capable of making through growth cycles, particularly the remarkable human capacity for plasticity in the adult brain. This leads some researchers to agree that the window of opportunity for learning, believed to be closed by youth is actually open for a much longer period (Diamond, 1988; Fischer & Rose, 1998). While early studies indicated a decline in intellectual capacity with age, attributed to loss of brain function, new research seeks to make the right connection between plasticity and the duration of the mental capacities of the aging (Tennant & Pogson, 1995; Diamond, 1988). Schaie attests to this fact through reports of the Seattle Longitudinal Study, which concluded that "cognitive decline is primarily not a result of aging itself, but as a result of the decade's long habits and patterns of behavior that we choose on a daily basis" (as cited in Heidemann, 2003). Heidemann says the good news about all of this is that the responsible culprits of decline are the behaviors that are mainly in our power to control.

Adult educators and others who have an interest in the literature and research of the neurosciences are finding that much of the older studies that rejected adult plasticity are being replaced by new findings which indicate the adult's ability to learn even into old age. The generally accepted knowledge of adult brain plasticity and the duration of intelligence is improving and making a difference in the approach to the connection between the development of the adult brain and the ability to learn (Diamond, 1988).

The old "Theory of Plasticity" that grew out of Kant's and Herbart's philosophy of education has gone through much change, we now know that the adult brain is able to cope with changes throughout the entirety of life, including learning new things (Sylvester, 1998).

As mentioned earlier, the concept of plasticity is not new but the scientific evidence of its occurrence in the adult's life is still a fascination to neuroscientists (Feyler, 1978). This information, coming from neuroanatomy, a subfield of neuroscience, has set challenges for the scientific field and for adult learning concerns. Feyler describes adult brain plasticity as the capacity to grow. The ever changing brain is capable of growing new circuitry rather than being a static structure that simply modifies the strength of its embryologically defined wiring pattern. This wiring, as discussed in an earlier chapter, begins after birth and continues into the adult life (1978).

Turkington (1996) believes the knowledge of brain plasticity is of utmost importance to those concerned with the study of learning. He points out that there are many ways to produce changes in the brain's synapses, such as electrical stimulation and neuronal disease, but enriched learning environments also have the same effect. This is worthy of the educator's attention. Ebner (1996) also believes these changes in the brain are due to learning, but he speaks of learning as the result of experience along with the storing of new information. It is commonly believed that changes in the brain through the modification of synapses occur easier in the child than in the adult, however new studies continue to give hope to adult learners. If the brain is stimulated, plasticity, according to Sylvester (1998), is kept alive. Baltes (1982, 1999) and others believe it has been proven through research that decline in plasticity in the adult brain can be reversed by special educational training. Baltes not only found that reversing decline in cognitive functions with adults was possible, but also that an amazing amount of untapped reserved plasticity can be found.

LeDoux (2002) explains how the reversal of decline is possible. He says new connections made by neural activity are subject to the "use it or lose it" rule as demonstrated in Fig.12. When new connections are made, only some survive; these are the ones that go on to be used. It is this use that prevents later loss; it is also what occurs between a postsynaptic cell and its presynaptic terminal that makes connections survive. Brain activity later strengthens these new connections. The Hebbian theory of plasticity holds that if two neurons are active at the same time, and one is presynaptic to the other, then the connection between the two will be strengthened.

Hebb's view of "fire and wire", which accounts for learning and memory, has also been used to explain other aspects of synaptic function, especially in the area of construction of synapses during development. Hebb suggested that in order to maintain increased efficiency of connections being made, between presynaptic and postsynaptic cells, new growth would always have to occur (LeDoux, 2002).

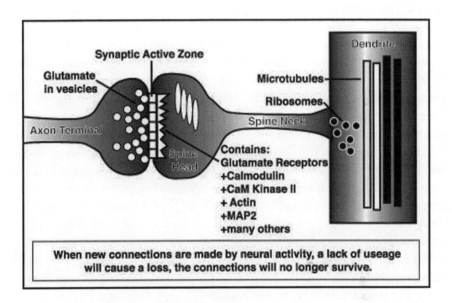

Figure 12 The making of new connections

Eric Kandel and a team from Columbia explain this growth as physiological plasticity which is accompanied by axon branching and new synapse formation both during development and learning. Once this branching and synapse formation occurs, a given action potential coming down the axon will be more effective in firing the postsynaptic cell. This causes more activation of synapses on that particular cell, and this activity induces growth restricted to the active terminals (LeDoux, 2002).

Postsynaptic receptors (NMDA) are very important as explained in the previous chapter, because they detect the match between activity in the presynaptic and postsynaptic neuron in order to cause growth. If anything disrupts these receptors or blocks them, then growth or development is disrupted (See Fig. 13). Neurotrophin, which is an important set of molecules, is also important for new synapse formation. Neurotrophin is a special tonic that promotes the survival and growth of neurons. When action potential occurs in a postsynaptic cell it causes the release of neurotrophin from the cell, which in turn diffuses backward across the synapse, where they are taken up by presynaptic terminals. Consequently, the neurotrophins cause the terminals to begin to branch and sprout new synaptic connections; only these active cells in turn receive molecules; and only they will sprout new connections. Through this process, active terminals grow (LeDoux, 2002). The NMDA (N-methyl-D-aspartate) plays the important role of detecting the match between activity in the presynaptic and postsynaptic neuron in the growth process.

Neurotrophins are also important in the prevention of cell death. When a new cell is created it normally seeks early exit. If presynaptic cells receive a life-sustaining shot of neurotrophins from its postsynaptic partner, cell death will be prevented. In other words, if there is a limited amount of neurotrophins, the survival rate of neurons will also be limited. The cells that are active are those that compete for neurotrophins; the ones that compete successfully are the survivors. These survivors produce or sprout new connections. LeDoux (2002) refers to this process as selection which he regards as a step along the way toward activity—in structured growth. Thus LeDoux apparently considers selection and instruction as partners in plasticity.

This knowledge of plasticity will help in answering questions regarding adult learning into late life. The questions posed by adult educators who have sought empirical evidence of adult brain modification and brain activity, proof of brain growth and the aptitude of learning new knowledge in old age (Sprenger, 1999), are dealt with in later chapters.

The following chapter speaks of increased plasticity created by the experiences of complex learning environments. It has been reported that our experiences change the structure of our brain, and the more complex the experience the more effective the change.

The NMDA (N-methyl-D-aspartate) plays the important role of detecting the match between activity in the presynaptic and postsynaptic neuron in the growth process.

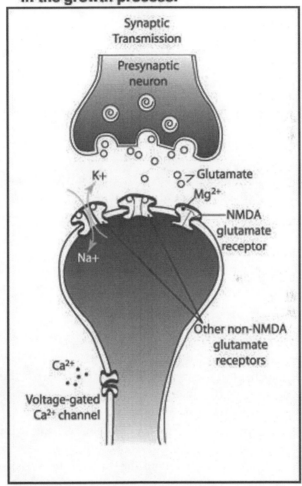

Figure 13 The NMDA

5

EXPERIENCE AND ADULT LEARNING

There have been numerous studies done on rats and other laboratory animals that have demonstrated neural plasticity because of an enriched learning environment. This was in contrast to animals who were left in cages that had nothing but the basic necessities. The animals in the enriched environment had toys and other stimulating objects, and the opportunity to socially interact with other animals. These research efforts have found that animals reared in a complex setting have exhibited increased synaptic contacts making them able to process and remember information more readily than other animals not given the same opportunity (Solomon, et. al., 1999)

There are biological changes that occur in the brain as a result of one's experiences. In 1997 Gerd Kempermann reported that mice reared in enriched environment developed significantly greater amount of neurons in the hippocampus (an important region of the brain affecting learning). These mice were able to learn a maze at a significantly faster rate than other mice. Researchers found that early environmental stimulation was very important. Rats that exercised experienced growth occurring in the lower region of the brain (cerebellum). It would appear that during early life certain critical regions of the nervous system develop, encouraged by environmental stimuli. This and other research has encouraged the toy industry to develop educational toys for children, because this brain stimulation at an early age is important. However, a continuing environmental stimulation is needed through life to maintain the status of the cerebral cortex (the thinking brain) (Solomon, et. al. 1999).

Adults possess a wealth of rich experiences that have helped in the development of their brains, this however must be encouraged through their life. Hiemstra (1993) believes the wealth of life and prior learning experience is one of the typical things adults bring with them to the educational endeavor. Cassara

(1993), in commenting on the differences between pedagogy and andragogy, said one distinction is that adults bring to education a mature mentality, experience, and the need to make decisions for themselves, their families, and communities. Early adult educators also saw the adult experience as being important to education. Rosenstock (Anderson & Lindeman, 1927) held strongly to the concept of life being the real school of the adult. He explained that for the adult, classroom theory becomes practical fact, and the practical facts which arise out of necessary experience are said to be backed by theory.

Cognitive neuroscience has now provided scientific support for andragogy's claims on the importance of experience for adult learning. Neuroscientists Elbert, Heim and Rockstroh (2001) from the University of Konstanz, Germany, have concluded that "Learning and experience affect the development of perceptual and cognitive abilities through mechanisms of reorganization of functional brain architecture, that is, through neural plasticity on a macroscopic scale" (p. 191). Elbert, et. al., sees promising evidence that experience improves skills. This they say may be happening through cortical reorganization. They consider the brain to be a highly dynamic organ which permanently adapts its functional and structural architecture to the needs of the environment. They conclude that every new experience makes us different (2001).

Bower (in Markowitsch, 2000), in showing the difference with adult learning, uses their experience to do so. He says that, by assumption, adult learners always come into any given learning situation with some knowledge, learning strategies and associations that they use to optimize performance on a given task. Bower believes that in many cases this is seen as a transfer of knowledge, the part of memory that exchanges information from short-term to long-term, used by the adult to help solve particular learning problems.

According to Restak (2001) a positive side of aging is practical experience and problem solving skills which tend to improve as the adult grows older. Restak also pointed out that it has been said that youth is "short on life and short on experience" while the opposite is true for the mature adult. This, he said, offers benefits to the adult learner, it helps to make up the problems that may be experienced when trying to learn new things and rapidly trying to access acquired knowledge. Restak also acknowledged that many age-associated difficulties can be conquered with experience.

Bransford, Brown and Cocking (1999) held that there are "alterations in the brain that occur during learning that seem to make the nerve cells more efficient or powerful" (p. 106). Solomon et al. (1999) agrees with Bransford et al. that animals raised in complex environments have proved to have a greater volume of capillaries per nerve cell than those who have been raised in a plain cage. The increased number of capillaries, which are tiny blood vessels responsible to supply oxygen and nutrients to the brain, provided these active animals with a greater blood supply to the brain. Bransford et al. concluded that this experiment shows that "experience increases the overall quality of functioning of the brain" (pp. 106–107), every new experience makes us different (See Fig. 14).

In view of the fact that the brain's structures are altered by experiences and that specific experiences seem to have specific effects on the brain, Bransford et al. (1999) says the nature of experience becomes an interesting question in relation to the study and investigation of the memory processes. When classes of words, pictures and other categories of information involving complete cognitive processing are used in the learning experience on a repeated basis, the brain is activated. This activation sets into motion the events that the brain encodes as a part of long-term memory. Experience becomes very important for the development of brain structures.

In understanding learning and memory it is particularly important to know that the mind imposes structure on the information available from experience. Overall, research confirms the importance of experience in building the mind by the modifying of brain structure. Just as practice increases learning, there is a similar relationship between the amount of experience in an enriched environment and the amount of structural change. Of great interest to adult educators, is the growing evidence that not only the developing brain experiences structural change from enriched complex environments, but the mature brain is also structurally altered when learning occurs. Findings by neuroscience are suggesting that the brain is indeed a dynamic organ which has been shaped to a great extent by experience. To be sure, the brain is built primarily by what a living being does and has done (Bransford et al. 1999).

Every new experience makes us different, aging offers many practical experiences and problem solving skills which only improves as the adult ages. Alterations in the brain occur through rich experiences making the nerve cells more efficient or powerful.

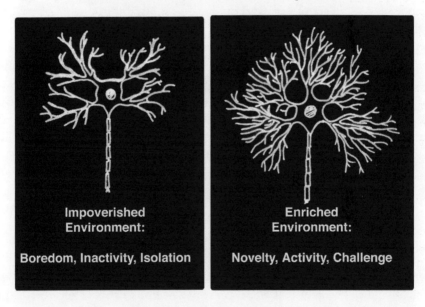

Figure 14 Every new experience makes us different

6

MEMORY RECALL AND ADULT LEARNING

Memory and recall are of key concern for aging adults, but they are not the only ones with an interest in the subject. Neuroscientists have for a long time shown keen interest in how it all takes place. Dowling (1992) commented that if neuro-scientists are able to understand memory and learning they will be close to pro-viding an overall theory on the functions of the brain. However, although we do not have all the answers Dowling thinks the past decades of research provide us with some understanding of how neurons are altered biochemically by synaptic input. These findings, he says, have led to important new concepts of possible conclusions underlying memory and learning.

This chapter examines the empirical research that provides insights into mem-ory and recall, the influence of aging and how this affects learning into late life.

MEMORY

Memory, like plasticity, also relies on chemical reactions and changes over the brain. Memory becomes real when groups of neurons network together in the same pattern after they have been activated (See Fig. 15). However, as we age, the average person finds that the ability to multitask and also learn complex new mental skills becomes less and less. Memory and cognitive function are declining with age and the deterioration of memory is not noticeable until the fifties. The memory lost includes visual and auditory; kinesthetic memory, however, remains mostly intact. Auditory memory will decline somewhat faster than visual memory until about age eighty, then visual memory begins to exceed the loss of auditory memory (Khalsa, 1997) (See Fig. 16).

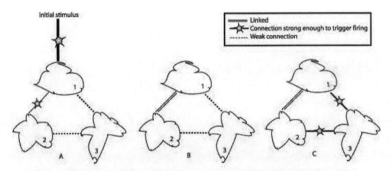

Memories are groups of neurons that work together in the same pattern
every time there is activation. Long-term memory must have more than one
brief situation, the more the better. This helps connections.

Figure 15 How memories are formed

Khalsa states that one apparent reason for this memory loss is the inability to encode memories as richly as young people do, using a variety of versions of each memory. This creates a problem for recall because there are fewer associations to bear-up or support each memory. Recall is difficult for some adults even when they are given associations in the form of cues that would normally trigger some memory.

"Memory" says Howard, et al. (2000), "is learning that sticks" (p. 525). Before memory takes place, potential new learning lingers briefly in a small area located in the right prefrontal cortex above the eye and one inch behind the forehead. This area of the brain holds the working memory or short-term memory until it is decided that we want to keep this information. When we decide to remember the important information, new synapses are formed and old synapses are then strengthened. The new synaptic connections are the new learning that takes place. When the branches of the brain cells have narrowed, learning has then occurred. If this is then converted into long-term memory the new information will stay. If this new information is not used it will disappear, just like a new muscle fiber breaking down if it is not used. For memory to stay it must be studied or rehearsed. The learner must practice new knowledge to prove an intention to keep. New knowledge must be filed; it must be placed in order. The learner must also show intention to remember by making an effort to remember (2000). Balles (as cited in Howard, 2000) said it well when he explained the process of memory as remembering what we most understand, and understanding what we choose to pay attention to and usually we pay attention to the things we want. Important to adult education is Russell's (1979) observation that there is little evidence to support research which concludes that memory decreases with age in the manner usually claimed. Russell says many studies are showing just the opposite (1979).

Russell (1979) pointed out that the brain learns better and more readily the things that are naturally more outstanding; for this reason it appears to deteriorate in older people. "In childhood", said Russell, "there are many more new remarkable and outstanding experiences than there are later in life, and these more 'special' events are better remembered" (p. 69). Russell suggests that the deliberate paying of attention to the present and the maintaining of an interest in the subject matter can lead to greater improvement of memory for adults.

Russell's (1979) conclusion adds credence to the concepts in this book of the adult being able to learn even into late life. He says:

> It is a common misconception that intellectual abilities necessarily begin to decline after the age of twenty. Neurologically speaking, there is no reason for abilities to decline: They should keep on improving throughout most of life. The apparent decline is probably due to (1) a lack of use; (2) an expectancy of decline. Recent memories can be enhanced and the apparent decline reversed if one maintains an active interest in the present (pp. 228, 229).

Multitask and complex new mental skills become harder than experienced at youth because memory and cognitive function are on the decline. Visual and auditory memory decline but kinesthetic memory remains mostly intact.

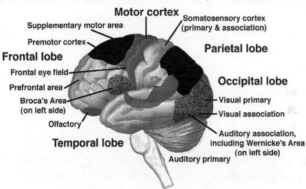

FUNCTIONAL MAP OF THE HUMAN BRAIN

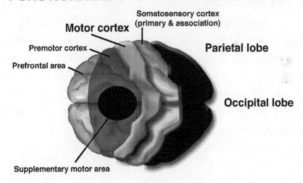

Figure 16 Functional map of the human brain

For clarity, the research conducted on memory is divided into two categories: firstly the declarative memory—memories revealed by way of intentional retrieval of past experiences, e.g. "what did you eat yesterday?" Declarative memory permits one to be able to distinguish between episodic memories, which are one's personal experiences, and semantic memories, which hold general facts, general words and their meaning. Secondly, nondeclarative or procedural memories are those memories that are manifested in subsequent behavior. This happens minus the direct recollection of any previous event. It is also considered implicit memory, such as how to ride a bicycle; one may not be able to explain the procedure, or when last they rode one, but can easily demonstrate the procedure (Balota, Dolan, Duchek, 2000).

DECLARATIVE MEMORY

Declarative memory, according to Restak (2001), may be defined as, "Knowing that" (p. 156). Restak explains that this includes the facts and events that make up life. It is the hippocampus and medial temporal lobe that appear to be most critical to the formation of declarative memory. Since the declarative memory includes both long-term and short-term memory, the frontal lobes are also considered important for developing ways to transfer information to the hippocampus, for long-term storage, from short-term and working-memory holding.

In declarative memory, researchers distinguish between memories that are episodic in nature such as personal experience, specific events, special settings, a given time, and memory that is semantic such as general facts, words, what words mean, names, and figures. It is believed that older adults, age sixty and over, have a much greater loss or disruption in episodic memory than in semantic memory (Balota, Dolan & Duchek, 2000).

Episodic memory.

This category of memory may be further broken down into other memory groups, namely: sensory, short-term or primary and long-term or secondary. Sensory memory is regarded as being raw information held for only a short time. Balota, et al. (2000) states that research shows very little difference between young adults, often college students at age twenty or so, and older adults. Short-term memory holds information in small amounts and there is an immediate awareness for a short period of time. A good example of this is knowing a telephone number and being able to hold this new number in the memory until it is dialed. Again, the literature on memory shows very little difference between the young adult and older adults in short-term memory. It is with long-term episodic memory that older adults show a difference in memory relative to younger adults. Balota, et al. says, the "deficits might occur at three distinct stages of episodic secondary memory: encoding…retention…and retrieved…" (p. 396).

Encoding is the initial storage of memory, but research is showing that even when information is presented in a rich manner, the older adult still has a problem with information storing. Retention is more difficult to isolate because of recognizable differences in initial encoding. Research shows that when initial encoding is equated there is little difference shown between young and old. The retrieval process shows great age related differences. It is even worse when cues are used to help with the answering of questions (Balota, et al., 2000).

Semantic memory.

Semantic memory may simply be referred to as factual memory. It is the memory that contains names of friends and acquaintances, words, meaning of words or use of tools and does not rely on time and location as a frame of reference (Greenfield, 2000). Carter (1999) defines this memory as the facts that are registered by the cortex and end up being encoded in the cortical areas in the temporal lobe. At a later time retrieval is carried out by the frontal lobes. Restak (2001) adds that these facts enter the cerebral cortex through all five senses but is only held for a fraction of a second unless given attention for a long enough period of time for it to be transferred to short-term memory. When transferred, this will only stay briefly and there is a limited capacity of about seven items at a time. Working memory takes this information and does something with it.

To store the necessary facts on a long-term basis, the information must be consolidated by repetition or application of the meaning. This, Restak (2001) says, triggers the protein synthesis which in turn locks in what would otherwise be only temporary brain connections. Restak states that most of what we commonly associate with the memory of names, facts, and figures involve structures on the inner or medial side of our temporal lobe. This, he says, includes the hippocampus, the amygdala and also the specific sensory pathways that receive the information. Balota, et al. (2000) uses the example of naming the author of *The Adventures of Huckleberry Finn* as a good question to test semantic memory, or "Isjrunsk an English word?" (p. 397). If one can answer easily and quickly to these questions it indicates a large reservoir of information well organized for rapid retrieval. Balota, et al. believes one's approach to the understanding of semantic memory is to assume that our knowledge is placed in an organized network of words or concepts referred to as "nodes". These nodes are connected to other related ideas by way of associative/semantic pathways. When nodes are activated by exposure to a particular fact, activation spreads from one activated node to other related nodes which are in the network. This makes them more accessible for needed processing.

Balota, et al. (2001) states that the principal task used to evaluate the semantic spreading activation is known as the semantic priming paradigm. Here two stimuli are presented sequentially and the relation between the prime stimulus and the target stimulus is manipulated. When related words are used, participants respond faster and are more accurate. These studies found that older adults either produce slightly larger semantic priming effects than younger adults. In some cases, the priming effects are similar. By this is meant that the time factor between the prime and target may be longer for older adults. However, if only the automatic response is being evaluated or measured in the older adult, the semantic memory network is said to be relatively intact. Examples given to this paradigm are the participants responses to a name or word that is semantically related to the first word given—doctor, nurse, or the strength association of things such as—strong: animal—dog vs. weak: animal—swan.

Other areas of age deficits in memory.

Other areas of age deficit in memory, according to Balota, et al. (2001) are:

1. Encoding Specificity—When encoding and retrieval tests were administered to young and older adults, it was concluded that the older adults are especially poor in the conditions in which there was a match between semantic encoding and semantic retrieval conditions. The operations seem to decrease in older adults compared to younger adults.

2. Memory for Context—Age deficits may also be seen in the secondary episodic memory in the area of particular details or the context of prior events. In some cases adults may remember content shared but may not remember who shared the content. Or the older adult may remember an event but not where it was nor when it took place.

3. Prospective Memory—Prospective memory is regarded as actions that must occur in the future, e.g. taking medicine every four hours. Then there are

those tasks that are event based, e.g. delivering an important message to a friend the next time you see him. "Time based tasks require more self-initiated retrieval processes and, perhaps not surprisingly...reveal the largest agerelated deficits" (p. 396–398).

PROCEDURAL OR NONDECLARATIVE MEMORY

Procedural or nondeclarative memory is described as being a broad category of happenings that clearly reflect memories of many prior events or episodes. This memory works without having to recall any explicit happening of the past. Balota, et al. (2000) says the best example of declarative and nondeclarative memory are studies done with amnesiacs, who have been observed to perform poorly on declarative tasks but relatively well on nondeclarative tasks. While there has been some age difference seen in the performance of nondescriptive memory task on occasion, the general conclusion is that any differences in performance in age is very small (2000).

Nondeclarative or procedural memory deals with specific sensory and motor pathways, according to Restak (2001). Also involved are the cerebella, the amygdala, and a few other brain structures deep in the white matter of the cortex. In both short-term and long-term memory, Restak explains that the thalamus provides the gateway for information gained by the senses and focused attention.

The summary of the empirical findings as related by Balota, et al. (2000) regarding memory changes in the aging, is that it is clear that most memory deficits experienced in the storage of long-term memories, such as, episodic memories and that of semantic memory, produce little age related change in performance.

RECALL

Working along with memory is the process of recall. Bransford, Brown and Cocking (1999) pointed out that the brain is actively at work both in storing and recalling information. This information is believed to be stored first in the short-term memory then sent to the long-term memory for recall at a later date. Researchers (Balota et al., 2000; Solomon et al., 1999) now believe that this information stored in the long-term memory is believed to remain there as long as the person is healthy. However, the problem faced by most adults is the finding of material stored. Solomon et al., (1999) suggest that one of the problems of recalling may be the incorrect search for stored information. Recall of information can be improved by new ways of storing knowledge. One such way, says Solomon et al., is through strong association between the items being stored. Markowitsch (2000) sees memory recall occurring when one includes various forms of evidence, made available to help with the storage of information. For instance, environmental conditions are believed to help influence the retrieval of information. Neuroscientists have found that the nervous system has stored an enormous amount of information which, without appropriate retrieval cues, only bits and pieces are available for recall (2000).

Cognitive neuroscientists believe there is a correlation between age, speed of acquisition and recall of short-term memory. Sensory impairments have been blamed since what is to be remembered must first be processed through the senses. For many adults the senses decline with age, especially sight and hearing. Also recalling information becomes slower as one ages for reasons already mentioned, such as, disuse, interference, physiological functioning and neurochemical activity (Balota, Dolan & Duchek, 2000; Darkenwald & Merriam, 1982).

7

INTELLIGENCE AND ADULT LEARNING

The connection between the aging process and the measure of intelligence is crucial for anyone who cares to understand how adults respond to new learning. If adults experience systematic changes in their intellectual functions as they age, it is of paramount importance that adult educators understand and respond to such changes (Tennant & Pogson, 1995).

THEORETICAL PERSPECTIVES ON INTELLIGENCE AND AGING

Aging, as observed by Restak (2001), begins in the 20's, as explained earlier. Research conducted by Denise Park, a Researcher at the Center for Aging and Cognition at the University of Michigan in Ann Arbor, shows that even at twenty to thirty a person tends to become a little slower. Information is processed slower, held shorter in the conscious awareness, and recall is less efficient. Restak says these changes are incremental beginning as early as the thirties. Aging experiences change in the brain first in memory. As we approach middle age more time is needed to learn new information. Along with this change is the amount of information that can be comfortably stored in the long-term memory. As a result, long-term memory becomes less reliable and more time is required to input this new information and retrieve the same information. Also, as we age it becomes harder to focus, keep to a particular point and filter out extraneous noise. This is most evident beginning in the late sixties to the early seventies. Many tests have been performed on older adults and young people to compare the difference in the speed of processing information. It is by these measuring tests that psychometric studies conclude the intelligence of adults in comparison to youth. Balota, et al. (2000) report that these studies use the approach of predicting mean response times of older adult subjects, from the mean response times of, over a set of conditions within tasks and also across tasks. When this is done, the result is a linear function accounting for over ninety percent of the age-related variance across a wide variety of measures.

The rate at which adults process information has for many years been the research interest of scientists in the field of psychometrics. While adult intelligence has been measured according to the speed of processing information; decline in the speed of processing information has been viewed as decline in intelligence.

Research conducted by Salthouse (1982, 1996, and 1998) and Lawton (1998) has argued that processing speed is a mediator between age and other cognitive functions such as memory. It has also been concluded by Salthouse that age does not predict the speed of processing information, however the processing speed of information may say something about the older adult's age. Balota, et al. (2000) points out that even though there is proof that older adults process information slower than the average young adult, there is concern that the general slowing perspective does not provide a clear enough account of the patterns of age-related deficits, or the lack thereof, in different components of memory performance.

Memory loss or cognitive decline in older adults has been used by psychologists as the measure of intelligence. Standardized tests first introduced in the late 1800's became the procedures used to record the speed of decline in cognitive abilities in older adults. These tests, according to Salthouse (1982), indicated that the component abilities included in the test of intelligence would exhibit distinct developmental trends in the adult.

A more elaborate descriptive system that arose out of the principal assumptions of a set cognitive decline in age, is the distinction between fluid and crystallized intelligence, a psychometric structural theory that was made popular by Horn, Cattell and Donaldson. These researchers have repeatedly suggested that developmental views of intelligence can be understood in the expression of a distinction between two major types of intelligence. As discussed earlier, fluid intelligence is expected to decrease as one increases with age. The other is known as crystallized intelligence, which is seen as the cumulative end product of all information acquired by the activity of fluid intelligence processes.

Salthouse (1982) holds that no generally accepted explanations have been given for the differential declines although many descriptions have been provided. Salthouse believes that the theories of fluid and crystallized intelligence are short in representing an explanation, mainly because they seems to be somewhat arbitrary and based primarily on the data gathered from observed developmental trend instead of *a priori* considerations. What is needed says Salthouse, is:

> Some means of identifying the neurological processes responsible for a given ability such that the classification of abilities into fluid and crystallized groupings could be verified with neurological observations (1982, p. 70).

Salthouse (1982) however does recognize Horn's speculation that fluid intelligence might be based on generalized, diffused neural activity while crystallized intelligence is derived from focused, specific natural activity (p. 70). This explanation, according to Salthouse, may be a start but is certainly not enough to explain the fluid-crystallized classification system in a neurological way.

Tennant and Pogson (1995) are in agreement with Salthouse (1982) on the point that early studies of the development of adult intelligence revealed a decline in intellectual capacity as one ages. This, says Tennant and Pogson, has been attributed to loss of brain function. They have documented similarities with the PMA (Primary Mental Abilities) test results, the WAIS-R (Wechsler Adult Intelligence Scale) test used for clinical assessment and the theory of fluid/ crystallized intelligence system. They conclude that research using standard intelligence tests all indicate some decline in intelligence, when older adults and young adults are compared, but only late in life. It has been established that where decline is found it can often be reversed through training. It has also been concluded that the components of intelligence based on learning from experience are maintained or even increased over the course of the adult's life. The results of these tests and theories may seem to be plausible, but the intelligence testing tradition has a number of shortcomings that may create questions regarding the existence of distinct adult forms of intelligence (1995).

The questions arising from research in psychometrics concern the true measure of adult intelligence, the possibility of increase, decrease and stability of intelligence; yet, if there is decrease with age, can education modify this? Neurology seeks to answer the questions concerning brain plasticity into old age, the chemistry of learning and memory performance in older adults, and the genes responsible for cognitive abilities. Neuroandragogy on the other hand seeks to bring the research in both fields together to achieve a better understand of the adult student.

The neurological definition of intelligence.

As observed in the response to the empirical research in psychometrics there is much dissatisfaction regarding the conclusions made about intelligence and the stability of adult brain plasticity. Salthouse (1982) calls for the examination of adult intelligence to be done by identifying the neurological processes responsible for given abilities. He suggests the neurological examination of memory span, induction and the acquiring of new information. This, he believes, will answer questions relating to fluid intelligence. Regarding crystallized intelligence he suggests the neurological examination of vocabulary, general information, comprehension, arithmetic and reason with familiar material. Kline (1998) also believes there is a need to move to a new level in the empirical research in psychometrics. He calls for an understanding of the physiological aspects of intelligence. A biological and anatomical study of the brain functions provides such information.

Since many scientists today suspect IQ measurements as being poor tests of human intellectual abilities, intelligence must be explained and measured differently. Susan Greenfield (2000) writes that:

> IQ does not measure the ability to understand or appreciate the significance of something or its meaning. This mental capacity to interpret objects, events or people in the light of experience might be equated more with wisdom—the wiser you are, the more meaning you see in life. Surely it is wisdom, not IQ, that makes humans so special (p. 141).

She continues by saying that wisdom is essential for successful living in the human world. She also adds that as human beings we depend on our experiences, not our genes, to give us the skills we need to survive. With the ability to learn from experience, human beings can survive in any corner of the globe (Green field, 2000).

To truly understand the biological makeup of adult intelligence, we must examine the effect experience has on the brain.

Experience and intelligence.

It may be true that the older one gets, the slower he or she is to respond to a task or a situation. However this has nothing to do with reaction time affected by age, in many cases, but rather time used by the adult to mull over situations, reflecting and drawing from life experiences to arrive at conclusive decisions. This, according to Denise Park (as cited in Restak, 2001), is why the government and large firms are not run by adults in their twenties, thirties or even their forties. Older persons, on the basis of extensive lifetime experience, are by far much wiser. Park says the older person can "put things into context, take a broader view, reach a decision on the basis of less information" (Restak, 2001, p. 162).

The intelligence of the adult does not decrease and abstract thinking and verbal expression remain stable. This stability experienced by the adult helps increase the expertise, professionally or otherwise. Park holds that any experience the adult brings to life situations make up for the lack of speed to respond to such situations because of the knowledge accumulated over the years (Restak, 2001).

Research is clear that adult intelligence is reliant upon how well the brain has been shaped by experiences through life. These experiences, which are gained in a variety of ways by adults, must be stored in the memory areas of the brain and made available for recall when the need arises.

As a result, Restak (2001) says the challenge for the aging adult is therefore one of maintaining healthy circuits and healthy synapses. Restak emphasizes the hippocampus and the nearby enthorhinal cortex. Both these areas, he says, are very critical to the formation of fresh memories and the bringing back of older ones. The brain uses all five senses to form memory; smell, taste, touch, hearing and sight are all gatherers of information and although much of the gathering is in tidbits, they are useful for memory storage. None of the information stored in separate regions of the brain exist in isolation, they instead form a composite of an integrated experience that's etched within the brain's synaptic patterns. When recall is necessary the experience returns in an integrated way, not in a 'hodge podge' of different sensory experiences.

Kaas and Florence (1996) make a similar conclusion regarding experience by saying that study on brain reorganization comes mainly from studies of the sensory systems. Sensory information they say is topographically organized so that it is orderly in its representation. We have gained much of our understanding of brain plasticity about adults from studying alterations of these orderly representations, mainly because their normal organization can be seen in great detail reveal ing even small changes. This sensory information, says Kaas and Florence, is processed largely within a hierarchical system which consists of interconnected neural centers represented in the brain stem, the thalamic and the cortical levels. This means, experience-dependent changes can occur to varying degrees at all levels. However, with the extensive studies of cortical representations, most of the evidence for the effects of experience on the organization of the brain involves cortical sensory representations. Kaas and Florence concluded that there is general agreement that experience does have a profound affect on the organization of the brain.

Bransford, Brown and Cocking (1999) are in agreement that experience increases the functioning of the brain. They say that different kinds of experiences will condition the brain in different ways.

Greenfield (2000) writes on the conditioning of Einstein's brain in an argument that holds that his was no different from the average brain in structure of function. Einstein was considered a genius. The question being asked by Greenfield and other brain researchers and educators is, what made Einstein's brain so special? When Professor Tom Harvey, a Pathologist at Princeton University and colleague of Einstein, examined his brain following his death, he found very little difference with that of the average healthy brain. Only two distinguishing features were found. First, in certain areas of Einstein's brain neurons had been better nurtured than normal. An unusually high proportion of glial cells were found in a region of the brain considered important for sophisticated thought. This difference was in ratio only, and the brains compared to Einstein's were fifteen years younger. Einstein died at seventy-six and as a result of age, his brain shrunk (2000).

The second difference noted was that Einstein's cortex was more densely packed with neurons than average. This allowed for the more efficient communication of cells according to Harvey. Although research shows contrasting results, that rats with neuronal dendrites spaced wide communicated better. Greenfield says a better explanation may be that at seventy-six Einstein's brain experienced the packing of neurons because the cortex gets thinner with age. Further research found Einstein's brain to be 1 cm (0.4 in) larger than normal on the left and right parietal cortex. Greenfield reasons that if Einstein's brain was normal but larger in these areas it must mean that some other area was correspondingly smaller. However, no mention of this has been found nor has there been any deficits reported in Einstein's mental portfolio, says Greenfield. It has also been claimed that one of the grooves in Einstein's brain (the Sylvian fissure) was much gentler than normal. This presumably allowed for more connections and better neural communication. Greenfield says, however, that a smoother cortex cannot be the key to intellectual agility or it would not be normal to have wrinkled cortex.

Greenfield (2000) states strongly that the physical shape and size of Einstein's brain had nothing to do with his intellectual prowess but instead the processes that occurred while his brain was alive. Greenfield calls this the "functional configurations that were generated" (p. 152). Greenfield concludes that to concentrate on a physical region of the brain, be it a single cell or single lobe, to understand brain power is wrong; it is better, he says, to examine the brain holistically. He agrees with anthropologist Terrence Deacon who argues that the size of the prefrontal cortex does not provide unique intellectual abilities, nor cell connections, but rather a balance of power between major regions of the brain (2000).

Yet there remain those researchers who wholeheartedly believe there is such a thing as general intelligence, biological and measurable with predictable elements of a successful life.

The biology of intelligence.

The biology of general intelligence is argued for by Linda Gottfredson in *The Scientific American Book of the Brain* (1999). Gottfredson, who believes intelligence can be measured accurately by IQ test also believes that general intelligence (g) is attained biologically. Gottfredson, however, agrees with critics that the concept of intelligence is really just a by-product of one's culture providing opportunities to learn skills and valid information fitting a cultural context. She says, however, that g is independent of cultural content, this includes beliefs about intelligence itself. She also holds that tests of different social groups reveal the same continuum of general intelligence. If this is the case, Gottfredson says, it means one of two things: cultures do not hold the responsibility of constructing g, or that they construct the same g. In any case, Gottfredson says, both conclusions would undercut the social artifact theory of intelligence which holds that intelligence is measurable.

Gottfredson (1999) believes that there is substantial research on the physiology and the genetics of g that has uncovered biological correlates of the psychological mysteries. Much of this study has been done both in North America and Europe and, according to Gottfredson, has linked several attributes of the brain to general intelligence.

However, Gottfredson says the existence of biological correlates of intelligence does not mean that intelligence is controlled by genes. Decades of genetics research may have shown that people are born with different hereditary potentials for intelligence and, in many cases, these genetic endowments seem to be responsible for much of the variation in mental ability among individuals. Gottfredson claims that the thought of IQ or the g being genetic and environmental in origin, as other psychological traits and attitudes, is not new to the experts. However, she says that the concept of hereditability of IQ rising with age is new. By this she means that the extent to which genetics accounts for differences in IQ among individuals increases as people get older.

An additional research finding that Gottfredson claims to be new is the finding that shared environments may have a modest influence on IQ in childhood but the effects dissipate by adolescence. An example given is, adopted children who seem to lose all resemblance to the adoptive family members, becoming more like the IQs of the biological parents they have never known. Gottfredson says there is still a lot of research being done to discover why siblings either do or do not share influential aspects of the rearing environment. Much of Gottfredson's conclusion came from the research of Dr. Robert Plomin.

Robert Plomin, a research professor of behavioral genetics at the Institute of Psychiatry in London, along with John De Fries of the University of Colorado's Institute for Behavioral Genetics and the Learning Disabilities Research Center, have collaborated to research the genes that may shape intellect. Their research has brought them to conclusions leading toward a theory that there are biological factors responsible for cognitive abilities as well as disabilities.

While it would be a natural thing to think of the environment as the source of differences in cognitive skills, that we are what we learn, or that we are products of our environment, Plomin and De Fries (2000) have taken a more balanced view; they prescribe to the concept of nature and nurture, both interacting in cognitive development. The past few decades of genetic research has pointed to a substantial role for heredity in forming the components of intellect. Scientists believe they are beginning to track down the genes involved in cognitive func tion. These findings are still new and Plomin and De Fries say they do not refute the old notion that environmental factors shape the learning process. What they do say, however, is that differences in people's genes affect the ease with which they learn.

Plomin and De Fries have largely concentrated their concerns on the verbal and spatial abilities. Their studies have included families with twins, both fraternal and identical. Adopted families have also been a popular family group studied by these scientists. Their conclusions are that differences of individual beings are related to the responsibility of genes. These studies are now claiming a modular model of intelligence which proposes that different cognitive processes are separated anatomically within discrete modules in the brain. These abilities are further seen as being genetically distinct, meaning genetic effects on verbal ability should not overlap substantially with genetic effects on spatial ability.

Plomin's and De Fries' search for cognitive genes has led them to examine rodents and insects wherein it is believed single genes related to learning and spatial perception have been identified. This has led to the investigation of mutations in single genes that may result in general mental retardation in the human population. They believe that more than one hundred single-gene mutations which impair cognitive development are now known. Normal cognitive functions, however, is orchestrated by many genes all working together, not by a single gene working in isolation.

These researchers believe it is important to stress that although they embrace the school of genetic effects on cognitive functions and abilities, they do not believe it means determinism is also genetic, nor do they believe that genes cause constraints on environmental interventions.

Howard Gardner (1993), a leading psychologist at the Harvard School of Education, and Daniel Goleman (1997), also of Harvard, both promote biological intelligence in their popular works. However, both authors question the efficiency of the IQ test as it relates to fair testing and both question the universality of g.

Gardner is well known for his works, *Frames of Mind* (1983), and later *Multiple Intelligence* (1993). Gardner wrote that the purpose of school is not to measure the abilities of the incoming student, but rather to discover these abilities known as intelligence and help in the development of such. This in turn would help them reach their vocational and avocational goals which, he says, would be appropriate to the individual's particular spectrum of intelligence. If this can be achieved, Gardner believes such people will be more inclined to serve the society constructively.

Gardner strongly protested against the theory of a universalistic view of the mind; rather, he held that a test designed to measure everyone in the same way through linguistic and logical-mathematical reasoning was not optimal. He wanted to consider skills like linguistic, musical, logical-mathematical, spatial, bodily-kinesthetic, intrapersonal, interpersonal and naturalistic abilities, which he dubbed "Multiple Intelligena" (See Fig. 17).

The traditional view of the definition of intelligence seems to be one's ability to answer questions on tests of intelligence. The results of the test scores are supported by statistical techniques that are designed to compare responses of subjects at different ages. The results are supposed to correlate with other test scores across ages and across different tests, which in turn corroborates the notion that general intelligence (g) does not change with age, training or experience. The grand conclusion indicates it is an inborn attribute or faculty of an individual (Gardner, 1993).

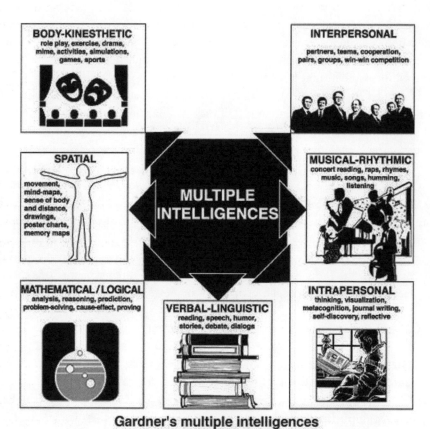

Figure 17 Multiple Intelligence

Gardner's theory of multiple intelligence simply pluralizes this traditional concept. For Gardner, intelligence simply entails the ability to solve problems or even fashion products that are useful in a particular cultural situation. This problem-solving skill will allow the individual to approach a particular situation in which a set goal is to be obtained and to locate the path to that goal. The cultural problems to be solved may range from creative story-telling to making the right move in a chess game or repairing a quilt (Gardner, 1993). Gardner makes a biological connection to intelligence when he says:

> MI theory is framed in light of the biological origins of each problem solving skill. Only those skills that are universal to the human species are treated. Even so, the biological proclivity to participate in a particular form of problem solving must also be coupled with the cultural nurturing of that domain. (Gardner, 1993, p. 16).

Language is used by Gardner (1993) as the most appropriate example of universal skill. This, he says, may manifest itself particularly as writing in one culture, oratory in another, and even as a secret language in others. Another example of a universal skill is mathematics and a third is picturing. These, Gardner thinks, are the three things that are universally used as symbols necessary for human survival and productivity. Intelligence, therefore rooted in biology, are separate and independent and cannot be tested fairly on IQ tests.

Daniel Goleman's book, Emotional Intelligence (1997), also examines another type of intelligence which may be classified as unconventional. Gole man's studies resulted from an interest in emotions and their effect on intelligence, as well as his rejection of the narrow view of intelligence that says IQ is genetic and cannot be changed by the experiences of life. Goleman claims that the explanation for the failure in life of people, said to have high IQ and the success of those said to have a modest IQ, must lie in the abilities he calls emotional intelligence: self-control, zeal and persistence as well as the ability to motivate oneself. Goldman holds that these skills can be taught to children, which in turn will give them "a better chance to use whatever intellectual potential the genetic lottery may have given them" (p. xii).

Pierce Howard (2000) believes interest and studies regarding the neurobiological correlates of intelligence will proliferate the twenty-first century. Three leading researchers in this area are Eysenck, Zuckerman, and Brody who hold that intelligence is the combination of the effect of hereditary and environmental contributions. Eysenck has claimed to find three correlates to traditional IQ in his neurobiological exploits, two of which are observed behaviors according to research. The third is a description of brain waves. Average Evoked Potential (AEP) is measured by the amplitude (height) of an electroencephalogram (EEG) wave. It looks at frequency, length of time—milliseconds, between waves and complexity of the wave.

Howard has listed the following as results of the studies:

1.   The more intelligent the subject, the more complex the wave

2.   The less intelligent the subject, the more variance there is across 100 tests

3.   In studies of high—and low—income children, the AEP has been shown to be more culture free, with less difference between classes than shown on the Wechsler Adult Intelligence Scale

4.   Facing familiar stimuli, higher IQ brains fire fewer neurons

5.   Facing novel, unfamiliar stimuli, higher IQ brains fire more neurons (that is, they bring more resources to bear) (p. 459).

Howard responds to this research by suggesting that people with higher intelligence relate mainly to speed—the traditional performance measures used by the IQ test. He would much rather think the best biological measure of intelligence is the quality of myelination. He says the thickness of the myelin sheath, its brittleness or flexibility is, and the effectiveness with which it grows are all associated within a mixture of intelligence measures. Howard holds that the quality of myelination is a function of one's diet, exercise and genetics (Howard, 2000).

Healthy older adults and IQ.

Although there remains numerous debates on the nature of IQ, its origin and development, Restak is very positive regarding the healthy, older adult and his IQ. Restak does not argue like Horn or Catell for measuring intelligence in old age by fluid measurements or crystallized measurements. He simply states that among other things such as language skills, vocabulary, abstract thinking, verbal expression, IQ remains the same. For Restak the older adult even gets better with age, and as a result, is given the responsibility to make the tough executive decisions. Restak's reasoning is that with age comes experience, with experience comes accumulated wisdom, with wisdom one may know how best to proceed in tough situations (Restak, 2001).

Restak (2000) states that the real challenge for older adults intellectually is how to keep the aging brain maintaining healthy circuits and healthy synapses, especially the hippocampus and the nearby enthorhinal cortex. This is because both areas are needed for the formation of new memories and recalling of old ones.

For intelligence to remain, the aging brain must also remain, plastic and stable. For this to happen, John Morrison (as cited in Restak, 2001) claims the aging healthy brain must keep neurons alive and make every effort to keep them communicating. It is also important that the synapses remain plastic causing new learning, which must be stable so that these new things learned will remain and not be forgotten. Morrison mentions the genes playing a roll in the securing of IQ into old age, but admits that not enough is known about it.

However, says Restak (2001), for the time being we must work with what we understand. So far, the most promising tools of maintaining IQ into old age is the synapse and the neurochemicals that influence it. Restak stresses the point made by Morrison that the synapse seems to be the site of aging and not the loss of neurons as once believed. Morrison points out that contrary to popular opinion aging isn't accompanied by a large loss of neurons. This being the case, the aging synapse is becoming a major focus for neurobiologists who have an interest in the neurological cause of mental decline. It is within the power of the older adult to maintain their intellectual powers by using what they have and stimulating the synapses by newness and novelties which cause the growth of new connections.

8

PSYCHOLOGY AND ADULT LEARNING

The most significant theoretical and empirical research relating to adult intelligence and learning ability occurred in the first quarter of the twentieth century in the U.S. This scientific research, called psychometrics, developed from psychology (Misiak & Sexton, 1966). Clifford (1973) in his historical report on American psychology said, "In 1931, at an international gathering of psychologists and educators, it was frequently remarked that America virtually owned psychometrics" (p. 243). The nature of psychometrics addresses concerns of adult learning, some adult educators believe this to be the scientific foundation of andragogy, the study of adult learning and adult education (Darkenwald & Merriam, 1982; Sav icevic, 1995).

An interest in the systematic study of learning in conjunction with aging inspired the emphasis of charting the changes that occur in intelligence, memory, thinking and creativity. This had much of its genesis in the German psychology of Wilhelm Wundt and other European psychologists (Darkenwald & Merriam, 1982; Misiak & Sexton, 1966).

PSYCHOLOGY

The beginning of psychology in Germany coincided with the development of andragogy. Draper (1998) explains that in the nineteenth and early twentieth centuries several forces were interacting in Germany which influenced andragogy in one way or another. Misiak and Sexton (1966), both historians of psychology, point to this period in German history as the beginning of psychology and its break from philosophy, becoming an independent science toward the end of the nineteenth century. This new science had strong effects on the education process in Germany, including andragogy (Darkenwald & Merriam, 1982; Misiak & Sexton, 1966).

It was German philosopher Johann Herbart who first identified the need and value of psychology to education before it became an official science in 1874. Herbart initiated the call for educators to incorporate the results of psychology. Misiak and Sexton (1966) consider Herbart as the true originator of educational psychology.

Psychology and psychological measurements.

Another area of interest is the psychology of Ebbinghaus, a German mathematician and psychologist with a special interest in memory. He brought together a very practical connection between psychology and education in general, while introducing statistical measures to psychology. This was later used in educational psychology for research and measurement. Ebbinghaus had a special interest in the quantitative study of the mental processes, particularly memory. This led to extensive interest shown by later scientists in learning and memory. Ebbinghaus' contribution to adult learning is found in his employment of statistical concepts and procedures.

This laid the foundation for research in adult intellectual abilities and learning including the measuring of intelligence (Misiak & Sexton, 1996).

T. L. Thorndike's *(1874–1949)* work in psychology also proved crucial to improving education, including adult education and learning research. Thorndike and J. B. Watson established behaviorism as a predominant school of psychology in the 1900's. Through their research, the nature of mental processes was first investigated. This theory had been speculated for centuries and was for the first time investigated in a systematic way. While Watson concentrated on the mind and mental activity as it relates to the behavior of individuals, Thorndike examined the measurement of mental ability and educational achievements, arriving at theories of learning (Darkenwald & Merriam, 1982; Gerow, 1992).

Thorndike's experiments and research in learning led to the first scientific work, of any psychologist, on the intelligence and learning ability of adults. His research and development of learning theories coincided with the introduction of andragogy to the U.S. While Anderson and Lindeman (1927) were writing about their discoveries of andragogy in Germany, Thorndike, in 1928, was making ground-breaking discoveries that would eventually give support to the new field of andragogy (Darkenwald & Merriam, 1982; Savicevic, 1995).

Thorndike's new findings supported the concept held by a few, that that no one is too old to learn. He was one of the first scientist to publicly declare that adults can learn. This was in contradiction to the theory which held that adults were not capable of learning new concepts. Thorndike however concluded that there were many factors other than intelligence that might significantly affect adult learning (Darkenwald & Merriam, 1982; Knowles, 1979).

PSYCHOMETRICS, THE MEASUREMENT OF INTELLIGENCE

The full development of psychometrics through the years affected andragogy, both positively and negatively. Empirical research methods were used that scientifically supported the theoretical positions advanced by andragogy (Savicevic, 1995). However, because testing methods designed for children were used on adults, and young cohorts were used for research, negative inductions on adult intelligence have been drawn.

Woodruff-Pak (1988) has outlined four main phases that cover the development of psychometrics in the U.S.:

1. Research in adult intelligence and learning;

2. Theories of fluid and crystallized intelligence;

3. Research in manipulation of adult intelligence;

4. Measuring adult intelligence with pedagogical instruments.

Research in adult intelligence and learning.

The prototype for contemporary intelligence testing was created in France in the early twentieth century by Alfred Binet and psychiatrist Theodor Simon. Their aim was to separate school children in Paris who had little cognitive capacity to learn from those who were considered normal. Binet and Simon's instrument, designed in 1905, measured judgement, comprehension and reason. This test was contextualized by Louis Terman of the U.S. to fit the American education system, and by 1911, it was being used to test adults (Woodruff-Pak, 1988).

The first adults tested by this newly modified test were soldiers of the United States Army during the First World War. The test was used as a method to screen out men who did not have the mental capacity to perform in the military. The test was known as the "Army Alpha Examination" (Woodruff-Pak, 1988, p. 315).

The scientific result, as reported by the U.S. Army, was that older adults performed more poorly than the younger ones. This was the first indication that a possible decline in intelligence occurred after the age of twenty. The range of comparison was 16–60 years of age; and as early as 25 years of age there appeared to be some decline. This statistic was published in 1921 by the National Academy of Science (Yerkes, as cited in Woodruff-Pak, 1988). In spite of new discoveries by investigators, the initial perspective of intelligence in adulthood and old age was established as one of decline. This conclusion affected research in the field of geropsychology and developmental psychology for over 30 years, because adults were incorrectly considered less intelligent than they really were (Woo druff-Pak, 1988).

R. R. Willoughby, in 1927, reported the first study on intellectual ability in adults. His study covered middle-aged adults as well as children in school. The result of his work revealed that different mental abilities were sharper with age. In a test of analogies, the youth performed better; but on the test of arithmetic, the older subjects did best. Willoughby concluded:

> Functions characterized by sharp peaks are essentially maturational in nature, acquired as a matter of normal growth and relatively free from influences of school training. Tests such as arithmetic and vocabulary, on the other hand, reflect accumulated experience and maybe relatively easier for adults. (Cited in Woodruff-Pak, 1988, p. 317)

E. L. Thorndike (1928) agreed with Willoughby's research on adult intellectual ability. Thorndike's conclusions were not popular, as he believed that adults were capable of learning and that intelligence did not drop significantly with age. Thorndike's methods however were cross-sectional tests of younger and older respondents, with results based on timed and/or motor tasks, including activities that may not have been meaningful to the participants ("learning to write with the left hand or memorizing an artificial language, for example" Darkenwald & Merriam, 1982, p. 105). This led to later criticism of his methods.

The studies of adult intelligence that followed Willoughby's and Thorndike's reports were published in the 1930's, 40's, and 50's. They basically concluded that if there was a decline in the intellectual capacity with age it must be attributed to the loss of brain function (Woodruff-Pak, 1988). Researchers noted the fact that the tests concluded during this era were cross-sectional and not longitudinal; that the subjects were being tested with an IQ test that may not have been valid; that the methods of testing were designed for children and not adults; and that these studies only measured generational differences in performance and, in turn, called those performances developmental changes. Some researchers were careful to explain the decline as a slow decline which may have only started in the 70's with a possible sharper fall thereafter (Belsky, 1984; Welford, 1958; Woodruff-Pak, 1988).

The inadequacy of the IQ test when used on adults caused Thorndike to object strongly to its use. By the early 1930's David Wechsler, in an attempt to address the shortcoming of the first IQ test, designed the Wechsler Adult Intelligence Scale (WAIS), specifically for the testing of adult intelligence. However, Wechsler himself was not convinced that intellectual function is not tied to the aging process (Darkenwald & Merriam, 1982).

This theory began to change when longitudinal studies, first published in the early 1950's, casted doubts on the notion that intelligence declines with age. The first published work is that of Owens in 1953, who did a follow-up study of the Army Alpha Examination in 1919. This was a 31-year follow-up of 127 men that predicted brain functioning would decline with age. Upon retesting, they proved to have gained over a half of a standard deviation. None of the subtests demonstrated loss of ability and some of the subtests even indicated statistically significant improvement. These results were explained away by critical scholars who still believed in the "theory of plasticity". Owen's study was replicated by Bayley and Oden's report in 1955 and the Oakland Growth Study in 1959. Both tests reported gains in intelligence and felt these subjects were exceptional because of the delay in decline (Woodruff-Pak, 1988).

Berger and Thompson (1994) criticized both the cross-sectional studies as well as the longitudinal. The cross-sectional, they said, may overestimate adult intellectual decline, showing low mental abilities when adults are compared with youth, not considering that most people improve in primary mental abilities throughout adulthood. Longitudinal designs may do just the opposite, that of underestimating the decline and showing great mental abilities when retested many years later. They caution that subjects may become very familiar with the test, thus improving their performance as they become practiced test takers (1994).

During this period of cross-sectional and longitudinal research, Raymond Cattell and his student John Horn, asserted a new theory of adult intelligence that moved research in the direction of training, educating, and then testing.

These researchers argued that there were two general types of intelligence, the fluid, or GF, and the crystallized or GC (Woodruff-Pak, 1988).

Theories of fluid and crystallized intelligence.

Cattell (1967) and Horn (1970), criticized the existing model of intelligence which was based on mental abilities between 29 or 120, this they considered too large a number. Also, difficulties arose in representing a large number of mental abilities in an orderly, consistent, coherent, and empirically sound fashion. As a result, Horn argued for the existence of two abstract compounds of intelligence, which encompassed various primary abilities. These two abstract components were crystallized intelligence (GC) and fluid intelligence (GF).

Fluid intelligence is measured by tests of complex reasoning, memory, object manipulation in space, inductive reasoning, attention and processing capabilities. It is defined as an individual's ability to perceive, remember, and think about a variety of basic information. Crystallized intelligence on the other hand is measured by vocabulary, mathematical ability, stored information, verbal comprehension, and abilities normally associated with experience and acculturation. Some researchers have defined crystallized intelligence as the mind's culture-based software (Birren and Schaie, 1985; Lawton and Salthouse, 1998; Lemme, 1999; Tennant and Pogson, 1995; Woodruff-Pak, 1988).

Manipulation of adult intelligence.

By the end of the 1960's, research shifted from descriptive methodology to experimental design. This research, performed by causal-analytic work, involved manipulation as a part of the experimental research. "The question of why and how much plasticity in aging generated a new intellectual climate of optimism," (Woodruff-Pak, 1988, p. 327), was the main concern. There was much talk about possibly interfering in the aging process by using intervention tools. These tools were already being used in the study of child development and intelligence. Researchers were also learning from development studies of younger age groups that "cohort differences in intelligence scores were often greater than age changes" (p. 327). Outside forces operating in the environment were often used to explain this cohort variable. From these findings, researchers reasoned, "that if environmental forces such as education led to differences in adults' intelligence test scores, manipulation of those factors should alter the scores" (p. 327).

By the end of the 1980's, there had been about fifteen published intervention studies on the manipulation of adult intellectual performance. Following the review of these studies, additional studies were conducted on the plasticity of adult intelligence (Woodruff-Pak, 1988). The results of those studies indicate that a recovering of intelligence to its former level of performance is the main concern of plasticity research; that, where decline is found, it can be reversed through training. In addition, mental decline, as a result of aging, was viewed as being reversible and, if given the appropriate environmental experience, one's intellectual performance could be restored to its previous level of competence (Baltes, Kliegl, Dittman-Kohli, 1988; Baltes, Sawarka and Kliegl, 1989; Berger and Thompson, 1994; Kausler, 1991; Kliegl, Smith and Baltes, 1989; Lawton and Salthouse, 1998; Salthouse, 1985; Schaie and Willis, 1986; Schultz and Salt house, 1999; Tennant and Pogson, 1995; Woodruff-Pak, 1988).

Measuring adult intelligence with pedagogical instruments.

Birren and Schaie (1985) asserted that research on aging and cognition must be reinterpreted within a theoretical framework that fits adult situations. They observed that cognitive measuring of mature and aging adults were still per-formed, using models designed for children and youth rather than for adults. This meant that the cognitive abilities of adults were being interpreted with a regression oriented bias (1985).

Woodruff-Pak (1988) concurs with research that suggests that one of the major limitations of research conducted between the 1920's–1980's was based on information about intellect in older adulthood. This finding was obtained by tests initially designed for youth and children. Research in the 1980's to 1990's took an interest in re-examining the psychometric approach in an attempt to determine the most appropriate tests of intellect late in life. Also, the external validity of traditional intelligence tests was questioned by researchers in the case of the maturing adult. Gisela Labouvie-Vief summed this all up by saying, "…adulthood is no longer to be seen as the cessation of growth and development (and, consequently, as the beginning of aging) but as a life stage programmed for plasticity and further growth" (as cited in Woodruff-Pak, 1988, p. 331).

Woodruff-Pak (1988) suggested that intelligence tests must be designed for adults. One of the tasks of researchers working in this field was to begin by using a pattern similar to that of Piaget, which entailed carefully observing the behavior of older problem-solvers to discover their unique approach. Woodruff-Pak referred to an example provided by Salthouse (1984) who found that experienced older typists were able to compensate for a reduction in their speed by scanning ahead further in the material, thus keeping up their performance comparable to younger experienced typists. Some researchers have started by searching for qualitative changes in adult intelligence. Among them, Woodruff-Pak mentioned that there were investigators who had already started to apply statistical techniques, such as factor analysis, to the psychometric intelligence data. This was done to determine if the factor structure and the quality of adult intelligence changes over time. Traditional cognitive tests have failed because they have alienated older individuals who see the tests as trivial, failing to involve cognitive operations that occur in daily thinking and problem solving (1988).

Birren and Schaie (1985) examined the testing problems related to research in the 1920's–1980's, and specifically the model of fluid and crystallized intelligence by Horn and Cattell. Birren and Schaie argue that this model has been gauged by models of inference coming from logical theory. These theories of formal logic have excluded the issue of the relationship of such formal models to the concrete demands of adult adjustment. Horn and Cattell's results depict an intellectual maturity particularly germane in youth or in educational settings. This test lacked validity when applied to more mature adults with significant life experience and was difficult to test in a non-academic situation (1995).

Birren and Schaie (1985) pointed out that it was Piaget who referred to the cognitive maturity of youths and their ability to move from the concrete to the hypothetical, which enables them to operate in a world of possibility rather than a world of reality. This makes the cognitive abilities of youths flexible as they are able to approach any subject matter from multiple perspectives (1985). Adults differ in this area. They are committed; youths are flexible in thought. Adults are a part of the real world and have life-long decisions to make, as well as careers to develop and children to raise. They must decide on one course of action and cannot depend on a multitude of possible alternatives. Researchers suggested that previous empirical research and testing of adults have been conducted on the pure logic of the adolescent's or youth's budding cognitive development and immature mode of thinking. Scales that have been used to measure the adults' mental alertness and abilities are those that have been primarily pedagogical in nature, aimed at an initial mastering of the particular cultural knowledge base. Adult life experiences generally cannot be measured or gauged by these tasks. Research on aging and cognition must be reinterpreted and done within a theoretical framework that has been proven to be appropriate for adult adjustment (Birren and Schaie, 1985).

Again, Woodruff-Pak (1988) raised the question of the external validity of tests designed to predict academic performance in a population that is suffering from relative educational deprivation. By the latter part of the 1980's, the quest for adult intellectual abilities, which develop over a life span had been initiated. Finally, says Woodruff-Pak, older adults are being assessed on the wisdom and experience they already possess.

Discussions in psychology.

Salthouse and Lawson (1998) show concern regarding the problems and issues related to the using of standard tests to measure adult intelligence. Other researchers also believe the principal problem of defining the concept of intelligence is creating other problems. These problems are discussed below.

First, measuring what is called intelligence in adults by Standard Test is not practical, according to Tennant and Pogson (1995). The two primary reasons given are; one, that the ST (Standard Tests) are too culturally specific and, as a result, cannot be used outside the Western school-based culture. Two, that they are constructed from problems and tasks which come from the context or the culture of schooling rather than from life experiences. Tennant and Pogson report that in "less developed" non-Western cultures it has been found that very sophisticated cognitive abilities exist among the inhabitants. In other research it was discovered that informal tests were taken with better score results than formal tests by adults. For example, adults shopping and using pen-and-paper to do their calculations did better in correct scoring than on a formal mathematical test of similar calculating.

Second, contemporary views render the IQ test culturally biased and lacking real variations in performance between informal and formal testing for a real-world environment. As a result, say Tennant and Pogson (1995), "There is a need then to distinguish between intelligence as an abstract, context-free capacity, and intelligence as the application of capacity in everyday life" (pp. 23 & 24). In acknowledgment of this concern, Baltes et al. (in Tennant & Pogson, 1995) distinguished between the "mechanics" and the "pragmatics" of adult intelligence. By mechanics they mean a person's processing of information and solving of problems at a basic cognitive level. Pragmatic intelligence, on the other hand, is seen by Baltes and his co-workers as the ability to apply the mechanics of intelligence.

Third, Tennant and Pogson (1995) say there is a difference between a typical test problem and the kind of problem people encounter in the workplace, at home and in the community. This was the concern of Salthouse (1982) who asked whether IQ tests were relevant for older adults since they were originally devised for children. He says this concern stems from the assumption that academic intelligence and traditional intelligence tests are not exactly the same thing as "real-world intelligence" (p. 71).

Fourth, the notion of intelligence declining with age has been found to depend on the abilities being tested across the adult life span. So whether intelligence stays the same or declines seems to depend upon the particular questions regarding a particular composite of abilities included in the Global Intelligence Test. It is obvious, according to Salthouse (1982), that test scores can be predicted when composed of Information, Vocabulary and Comprehension. These will be fairly stable across the life span. However, questions dealing with Digit Symbol, Picture Arrangement and Object Assembly will have lower scores the older the participant and higher scores the younger the participant. For this reason Salthouse says:

> Global measures of intelligence are thus simply not suitable for analyzing adult changes in intellectual behavior because the nature of the function for the global measure is completely dependent upon the particular combination of subtests included in that intelligence scale (p. 70).

Salthouse (1982) says this argument implies that the relationship between age and the intellectual ability of adults is believed, by Salthouse, to exceed any other age-related limitations in most real-life decision contexts.

Sixth, the question of plasticity (Lawton & Salthouse, 1998; Baltes, et al., 1989, 1988) in adulthood has been posed by researchers in the field of intellectual development, who use various methods of research to explore this question. Baltes, a student of K. Warner Schaie and noted scientist in the field of psychometrics, elaborated Schaie's criticisms of the methods being used to measure adult intelligence. Baltes found several faults in the designs being used, such as: "selective sampling, selective survival, selective dropout, testing effects and generation effects" (Woodruff-Pak, 1988, p. 321). Baltes felt that these biases mentioned above could account for major discrepancies between the cross-sectional and longitudinal information given on intelligence tests.

Baltes and other researchers finally concluded that one of the major limitations with intelligence tests for adults is that all perspectives derived from information regarding intellect, are based on tests initially designed for children. As a result, psychometrics has been measuring adult intelligence with a yardstick designed to measure children and if adults deviate from the pattern of the young they are labeled deficient (Woodruff-Pak, 1988).

Researchers, since the early 1970s, began various programs that would begin to examine the adult no longer as one who goes through "the cessation of growth and development (and, consequently, the beginning of aging) but as a life stage programmed for plasticity and further growth" (Labouvie-Vief, 1985, p. 501 in Woodruff-Pak, 1988, p. 103). Other researchers in agreement say, "Adulthood can now be legitimately viewed, not as a period of intellectual stability or decline, but as a period of ongoing intellectual and cognitive growth, qualitatively different from childhood" (Tennant and Pogson, 1995, p. 34).

New research investigates the qualitative differences or changes experienced by adults in intellectual and cognitive ways using available data and measuring instruments, even novel methodology (Woodruff-Pak, 1988).

One such method has been the investigation of plasticity into old age, using the hypothesis that:

> ...older persons, on the average, have relatively little test experience and everyday practice in fluid intelligence, but that they possess the reserve—the latent competence—to raise their level of performance on fluid intelligence tasks to that of younger adults (Lawton & Salthouse, 1998, p. 102).

This research, when conducted using cognitive training, showed strong evidence of sizeable plasticity in the aging adult. Plasticity of intelligence became important knowledge to those researching intellectual graduation during adulthood. Researchers soon went beyond a search for range and limits of trained individuals, and how well they function, to a search for limits and boundaries of graduation. No longer are researchers seeking to find the normal range of intellectual functions in adulthood but rather their limits of performance (Lawton & Salthouse, 1998).

As explained earlier, Baltes and others (Kliegl, Smith, Baltes, 1989; Baltes, Kliegl, Dittmann-Kohli, 1988; Schaie & Willis, 1986; Baltes, Sowarka & Kliegl, 1989) took the lead in exploring the different aspects of plasticity and the boundaries of plasticity calling this examination "testing-the-limits". This is the predicting of developmental differences that are most pronounced, maybe irreversible, and near levels of maximum performance. It is believed by researchers that age changes are easily masked or modified when they are studied within a normal range of functioning. Testing-the-limits research has changed the focus regarding plasticity of intelligence, the task no longer focuses on the demonstration of plasticity as the center of development, but rather it is now a search for potential or reserve capacity and constraints.

9

HISTORY AND DEVELOPMENT OF ANDRAGOGY

THE ROOTS OF ANDRAGOGY

The majority of those who have researched andragogy agree that the principles of lifelong learning are a reflection of the ideas and teaching habits of a number of ancient philosophers and teachers (Henschke, 1998a; Savicevic, 1991).

In the ninth-century-B.C. Hebrew prophets did not view learning as merely the passive reception of transmitted content from teacher to student (Henschke, 1998a), rather as a process of active mental inquiry. Henschke (1998a) notes that Jewish Rabbis had the same view. Their schools developed the teaching practice of asking questions and answering by asking more questions, hoping to improve insight or to further investigate the truth of the matter. According to Knowles (1990), the Hebrews have also been credited with helping to establish what is now called the "case method," in which a facilitator or group member describes a situation, possibly in the form of a parable, and then together with the group the leader explores its possible resolutions.

The fifth-century-Chinese demonstrated an understanding of lifelong learning (Savicevic, 1991) through the teaching practices and philosophy of Confucius (551–478 B.C.). European thinkers were so impressed with the work of Confucius and with his scholarship that they described him as the "patron saint of the Enlightenment" (Dawson, 1981, p. 5). Confucius devoted himself to the private teaching of adults, preparing them for civil service examinations. His devotion to teaching and use of effective methods earned him the elite title of "Master" and he was subsequently credited with starting the first university (1981).

The Greek philosophers Socrates, Plato and Aristotle all demonstrated an understanding of the concepts of lifelong learning and principles of andragogy through their belief systems and practices. Savicevic (1991) describes their philosophies as ideas, thoughts and views that contained the concept of learning throughout life and the peculiarities and manner of acquiring knowledge in different stages of life. Russell (1972) characterizes Socrates (469–399 B.C.) as a teacher of adults. Full of enthusiasm, he first accumulated knowledge for himself and then imparted it to his students, the most renowned being Plato.

Plato (427–347 B.C.) became arguably the most influential of all philosophers (Gutek, 1995) and demonstrated his educational philosophy of lifelong learning in the system he called the Utopia. This concept favored the teaching of music and gymnastics for children ages six through eighteen. Students eighteen through twenty-one years of age underwent military training, and those who were twenty-one to thirty studied liberal arts. It was required of all future political and military leaders to complete five or more years of school. Plato designed his educational system for the elite and not the masses; however, his theories were not restricted to formal schooling but permitted informal learning tailored to the respective student's cultural context. Plato's assertion that knowledge is acquired through life at different phases in different ways directly affected these concepts of andragogy (Draper, 1998; Gutek, 1995).

Aristotle (384–322 B.C.), a student of Plato's, developed an educational system that was similar to Plato's. Like Plato, he believed in lifelong education. Aristotle's educational system begins in a systematic, formal way up to age twenty-one. Following this benchmark, the adult must be involved in theoretical and speculative studies, to include logic and metaphysics. Aristotle's educational philosophy has impacted Western scholarship and helped to shape adult education in both secular and Christian institutions (Gutek, 1995).

The historical bases of the concepts of lifelong learning and andragogical principles are also traceable to ancient Roman education. Cicero (106–43 B.C.) and Quintillion (A.D. 35–95), both Roman educators, developed teaching theories that addressed students' needs beyond youth and childhood. The two men encouraged continuing education, which included poetry, drama, prose, history, law, philosophy, and rhetoric. Many current problems faced by adult educators were addressed long ago by these early educators. These problems include theoretical and practical quandaries inherent in the process of teaching and learning, as well as the concept of learning readiness. The students' ability to comprehend the advantages of group work, and the development of social skills (Gutek, 1995), was also examined.

The foundation of andragogy and the philosophy of lifelong learning are very visible in the life work of Jesus Christ of Nazareth (4 B.C.–A.D. 29). Many adult educators have paid keen attention to the teaching practices and methods used by Jesus to impart His message. Barclay (1961), makes several observations pertaining to the success of the teaching practices of Jesus: (a) His teaching had universal appeal, (b) He spoke with an ability to retain the attention of his audience, (c) He implicitly understood the needs of the people and taught them accordingly, (d) He presented His lessons in a way they would be permanently remembered by His listeners, (e) He changed lives with His teaching, and (f) He inspired learning through life's experiences, using parables and spiritual truths.

These and other practices demonstrated by Jesus have gained the attention of adult educators who believe that many issues faced by modern andragogy were addressed in the educational practices of Jesus. Knowles (1970), Henschke (1998a & 1998b), Barclay (1961), and Mayer (1967) agree that such practices as teaching in small groups, training educators, promoting lifelong learning, and using adult teaching methods are important to the practice of adult education.

The philosophy of lifelong learning can also be traced to the concepts and practices of the medieval church leader John Comenius (1592–1670), whose philosophies made significant contributions to education in the seventeenth century (Gutek, 1995; Mayer, 1967). Savicevic (1991) goes so far as to claim that the conceptual heritage of Comenius gives us grounds for regarding him as the originator of andragogy, although his educational concepts were not called by that name. In his writings, Comenius expresses his belief in the vast importance of life and learning. He urges the establishment of special institutions for learning, the training of teachers, and the development of methods for working with adults. This approach, according to Savicevic (1991), is the root of the modern concept of andragogy.

The educational philosophy promoted by Comenius was shared by the Marquis de Condorcet (1743–1794), a French nobleman elected secretary of the Academy of Science and a leading member of the French National Assembly. The Marquis de Condorcet introduced a national plan for organized adult education and on April 20, 1792, proposed a plan for the systematic education of adults to the National Assembly:

We too have noticed that education (instruction) should not cease at the moment an individual leaves school but rather education should proceed throughout one's life and there is no age in which it is not useful and possible to learn; and this second educational period is all the more important due to the limited amount of education that can take place in one's youth. (Matzah, as cited in Pirtle, 1966, p. 11)

Although the Marquis de Condorcet was unable to implement his educational plan due to imprisonment and subsequent execution, Pirtle (1966) notes that his lifelong learning philosophy lived on.

ANDRAGOGY AND ITS DEVELOPMENT IN GERMANY

Organized learning in adult education was not experienced in Europe until the eighteenth century. Germany however did not adapt to organized adult education until the nineteenth century. This was brought about by social, economic and political changes. The Germans eventually developed their own institutions which provided organized education for adults (Pirtle, 1966; Knoll, 1981). However, within the years that followed there was great dissatisfaction with this new approach to adult learning and education. There was a sense that adults were being taught like children and were not learning how to cope with unfavorable social, political and economic circumstances. There was a need for a new approach to adult learning, and by the 1820's the rigidly organized method of adult education was being challenged.

THE BIRTH OF ANDRAGOGY IN GERMANY (1833)

Alexander Kapp, a high school teacher in Germany and an instructor for the workers' movement, initiated the concept of andragogy in his country in 1833. This move addressed the need for a new approach to the education and learning of adults (Savicevic, 1995, 1999).

Andragogy, for Kapp, was an important concept intended to make a clear distinction between the teaching of adult students, as opposed to pedagogy, the teaching and learning of children. Kapp chose the German word *andragogik*, a derivative from the Greek noun *anew*, the genitive case being *andros*, meaning "adult." Kapp was strongly influenced by the ancient Greek philosophers, especially Plato. Kapp concluded that adults needed education through philosophy and rhetoric, not science, gymnastics and art (Draper, 1995; van Gent, 1996).

Opposition to andragogy.

Kapp's *andragogik* met with great opposition from German philosopher Johann Friedrich Herbart (1782–1841), who thought it wrong to accept this innovative system because it would lead to a general dependence on the part of the adult, causing a permanent state of adolescence (van Gent, 1996). Herbart, a philosopher and professor of Pedagogy at the University of Konigsberg, Germany, was a student of Immanuel Kant (1724–1804). Kant's lectures on pedagogy made his position on the limitations of adult learning clear. As mentioned earlier he taught that education should not continue beyond sixteen years of age, and that the ability to learn new concepts should be fixed at about age twenty. Kant's pedagogy had taken deep root in German classical philosophy, and eventually developed into a theoretical and practical science (Savicevic, 1995).

Both Kant and Herbart "designated pedagogy as a science on the education of children" (Savicevic, 1995, p. 5). They insisted that only the young be offered the systematic method of education they advocated, one that occupied a particular time in life with a clear beginning and end. From this philosophy came the tradition and "theory of plasticity" that "perpetuated the idea that adults could not learn, physically or intellectually, after a certain level of maturation" (Birren, 1988, p. 4; Savicevic, 1995).

The impact of Herbart's influence caused the use of the concepts of andragogy to cease for almost one hundred years in Germany. Herbart's (1864) position was later published in his theses *Padagogische Schriften* (Educational Writing) (Knowles, 1990; van Gent, 1996).

Herbart's attack on andragogy did not completely bury the concept, as vestiges could be found in Russia around 1885 and in Austria in 1910 (Savicevic, 1991, van Gent, 1996). By the early twentieth century, according to van Gent (1996), a modest revival of andragogy occurred in Germany. Savicevic (1991) has mentioned several German authors who, in the early 1900's, attempted to relay the foundations of andragogy: K. G. Fischer, W. Flinter, C. A. Werner, W. Picht, R. Edberg, and E. Rosenstock.

Andragogy after World War I (1919–1945).

After the end of World War I, adult education spread rapidly throughout Germany, particularly in the workers' movement. German historians regard this period as "The New Direction of the Adult Education Movement" or the "Neue Richtung" (Pirtle, 1966, p.188, Reischmann, 2004, p.4). During this time, Germany experienced fifteen years of democratic adult education when 'The Protestant Workers' Association' committed themselves to socio-political engagement and became involved in the union movement, thus giving the Weimar Republic the support needed for the education of the workers (Pöggeler, 1996; Röhrig, 1990).

Around this time the University of Frankfurt found it appropriate to support and house a labor academy, and in 1921, the Academy of Labour was begun. This organization was an innovation in adult education under the Prussian Ministry of Science, Art, and Adult Education in cooperation with the labor union. The Academy functioned as a university college for workers without the necessary academic preparation, but with an interest in college training and accepted only mature students, 25 to 40 years of age, with varied life and industrial experiences (Hansome, 1931; Pirtle, 1966).

Eugene Rosenstock (1888–1973), the Academy's first director, immediately saw the need for a theory-oriented concept (Reischmann, 2004) that would fit this unique group of students. Rosenstock selected the concept of "andragogik" to represent the discipline he used in teaching these adults (Anderson & Lindeman, 1921; Hansome, 1931; Knowles, 1990; Savicevic, 1991, 1995; van Gent, 1996).

Rosenstock, like Kapp, found pedagogy to be inadequate for adults. For him there were three main propositions inherent in andragogy: (a) The adult worker is in possession of a surmountable store of ideas, experiences, concepts, daily knowledge, wrong information, and chaotic accumulation. While this barrage of information is often not well coordinated or verifiable, it is held together with a tenacity developed from much struggle and pain. Adding to the confusion, the adult worker notices a discrepancy between principle and practice; (b) the adult worker's mind operates best in an atmosphere of differences, contrary to what he believes. He is more alert where he meets a conflict of ideas. Thus, debates, criticisms, discussions, and opposing views stimulate the best learning; (c) to learn the new ideas, the adult worker must first eliminate the old untenable ideas and the notions so cherished. His best learning takes place through a living interchange of the thought process (Hansome, 1931).

Rosenstock also held very strongly to the concept of life itself being the school of the adult. This concept of andragogy was theory becoming practical fact, and the practical fact which arises out of necessary experience is backed by theory (Anderson & Lindeman, 1927).

It was in this period that Germany first consciously recognized adult education as a legitimate research field. In this era, many new institutions related to adult learning came into existence, causing many of the old educational societies to lose their clientele (Knoll, 1981; Pöggeler, 1992). Franz Pöggeler (1996) referred to this period as the time of democratic adult education. Pirtle (1966) documents that during the "New Direction," there was also a noticeable shift away from adult education as an instrument for massive social change to that of a technique for enhancing the development of human qualities and life's potentials therein (1966). The constitution of the Weimar Republic supported the adult education movement. Paragraph 148 of the Constitution, Section 4, states, "The populare education (Volksbildungsween), including the folk high schools (Volk shoehshulen), shall be improved by the National Government, the Federal Government, and the Local Authorities" (Weinberg, 1991, p. 129–130).

National socialistic education.

Germany's chance of becoming a democratic nation domestically, while remaining politically engaged internationally, was spoiled by the world economic depression that began in 1929. Germany's President, Paul von Hindenburg, had only one chance of continued survival—the formation of a parliamentary government. This would only be possible by accepting the support of the National Socialist Party. President Hindenburg made Adolph Hitler chancellor in January 1933. Three months later, Hitler gained dictatorial powers (Pöggeler, 1996; Schmelzer ed., 1978).

The adult education movement was greatly affected by Hitler's government. Many adult education organizations and institutions were ordered closed because they ran counter to the spirit of the "'New Nazi'" ideology. Political and intellectual plurality were considered impossible and adult education was renamed "'National Socialistic Education," or "people's education." The new educational system was considered fascist and remained in existence until the end of World War II (Pöggeler, 1996; Schmelzer, ed. 1978).

Andragogy after World War II (1945–1989).

In the period following World War II, adult education in Germany went through noticeable changes. There emerged differences in educational terminology and varied schools of thought as Germany became democratized and was integrated into the new educational system with the attendant introduction of new educational strategies. A greater degree of professionalization in andragogy was attained, with universities adding andragogy to their programs. This progress created a setting for the establishment of andragogy as a discipline (Knowles, 1970; Savicevic, 1991).

German Democratic Republic.

The German Democratic Republic (GDR) of East Germany was able to establish andragogy as an independent branch of its educational system after World War II. Before this, andragogy was treated as a sub discipline within the framework of general pedagogy. In 1946, a decree was passed by the supreme chief of the Soviet Military Administration to encourage the establishment of democratic adult education. This decree instructed the government to:

> ...disseminate among adults and young people general scientific and general political knowledge, to contribute to raising culture in general and the educational level of the public at large, and to educate the population in the spirit of democracy, antifascism and antimilitarism. (Schmelzer, ed., 1978, p. 11)

This decree was followed by the opening of new People's Universities in large towns and several small communities. In the industrial regions, "technical enterprise schools" were established. These instructions later became known as "enterprise educational centers for adults," and had a broad educational profile. This move to increase training and educational opportunities for adults was part of the plan Russia developed to improve its own socialist economic basis. In the first five years of the GDR, for example, an important new training measure was implemented with the goal of increasing labor productivity. Workers were expected to go through continuous training and education, a regimen that became a trade mark of the socialist society. For the soviets, there would always be a close connection between progressive economic, social and political achievements on the one hand and the improvment of adult education on the other (Schmelzer, ed., 1978).

These new schools needed instructors, and so adult education in the early years of the GDR concentrated intently on the training of new teachers. If this young state was going to be free of the old educational system of Nazi ideology, a new system of education would also be a necessity. It was therefore decided that management of education would be centralized, and based primarily on the Soviet Union's existing experience (Schmelzer, ed., 1978). Accordingly, in 1965, a law was passed to unify the educational system from preschool to institutions of adult education. This law also had the effect of underscoring the communist government's belief that adult education should be seen as an indivisible part of a unified system of education (Schmelzer, ed., 1978; Savicevic, 1981).

Organizationally, the GDR's adult education system had a varied base. A sharp division existed between the "school system" (formal education) and the "out-of-school" system (informal education) of adult education. The first system involved secondary vocational schools, "folk" high schools or People's Universities, academies of business and industry, village academies, and institutions of higher education. The second system involved adult education only and was developed by the Society for Propagating Scientific Knowledge. This organization provided education through cultural centers, clubs, theaters, museums, cinemas, libraries and the mass media (Möhle, 1990).

Educational officials of the GDR recognized very soon after the inception of its system of adult education that it would take adult educators with specific academic background, and level of familiarity with the practice of adult education, to handle the rigid curricular structure they had in mind. This understanding led to the systematic training of personnel in need of ideological education, and training that was professional and methodical beginning just after 1958. The East German adult education system chose to employ the instructional methods used in childhood education schools to present the methodology and didactics of adult education with special attention paid to relevant aspects of adult learning. Training would take place at the Universities of Leipzig and Dresden, as well as at Karl Marx University in Leipzig. There were three areas of training: the systematic and historical pedagogy of adults, didactics and special methodics, and the pedagogy of adult advanced training (Knoll, 1981; Savicevic, 1981).

Educators of the GDR carried out research and theoretical work in the field of adult education, creating a firm basis for training personnel and developing a system of educational science linked to the needs of society and the individual. Adult pedagogy formed the basic conceptual framework of this research which carried the specific subdivisions of business and industrial pedagogy, higher educational pedagogy and military pedagogy. East German officials eventually established a whole system of disciplines within adult pedagogy, overcoming the heretofore limited perception of adult pedagogy as a single discipline and a branch of pedagogical sciences (Savicevic, 1981).

The Federal Republic of Germany.

The Federal Republic of Germany (FRG), which was zoned to the west at the end of World War II, developed its own democratic adult education program.

Like the GDR, it was able to establish andragogy as an independent branch of educational science (Knoll, 1981). In 1947, the Allied Control Council gave the directive to adult educators to be responsible for "training active helpers for the democratic education of Germany by making the latest social, political and scientific knowledge accessible to the adult population" (Pöggeler, 1975, cited in Zdarzil, 1990, p. 84). This was an important task for adult education because there was still a disjuncture between the people and acceptance of the new democratic state. The FRG found America, England, and the Scandinavians countries to be good examples of democracy and adult education and used them as their basic model (Zdarzil, 1990).

Further developments in German andragogy (1989)

The German concept of andragogy did not develop in a homogeneous way but rather was shaped (at least in part) by the many wars, revolutions and political upheavals which punctuated the country's history. The frequency of these disturbances brought about new styles and systems of adult education which were not given sufficient time to develop and be tested before being disrupted by further national outbreaks (Pöggeler, 1996; Savicevic, 1991).

The general concept of andragogy in Germany encapsulates the science which concerns itself with the study of educational activities pertaining to adult education, development and learning. The subject being studied is the adult and the circumstances in which his/her education and his/her learning are occurring, regardless of learning circumstances, social, individual, organized or self-oriented, as long as learning and education take place (Savicevic, 1989).

The essential function of this interpretation of andragogy is the study of the development of education and adult education in both its formal and informal forms. Andragogy also focuses on adult development, intellectual, social, and psychophysical. The task of andragogy also includes the study of both the individual and the socio-philosophical and historical aspects of adult education (Savicevic, 1989).

The difference between Andragogy and Pedagogy in Germany.

In German andragogy there is no universally accepted standard for an age of maturity, but the most commonly accepted age is eighteen. As such, andragogy studies the education of human beings from late adolescence to death (Savicevic, 1989).

F. Pöggeler (1999) was the first theorist to attempt to provide andragogy with a scientific foundation. His efforts, which began in the mid 1950's, have resulted in almost a half-century of historical, theoretical and empirical research. Because of Pöggeler's work, andragogy in Germany has evolved into a scientific system separate from the disciplines of pedagogy. According to Savicevic, "A whole system of specific scientific andragogical disciplines have been constituted within the framework of andragogy, equaling or transcending, by its scope, the system of pedagogical disciplines" (1989, p. 10). Other German authors and educators (Knoll, 1998; Reichmann, 1993) agree that andragogy is to be accepted as a discipline with its own sub-disciplines that constitute a new branch of educational science that can no longer find a place as a sub-theory of pedagogy.

Kapp (1833), held that *pädagogik* was distinctly meant to educate the minds of the young; *andragogik*, on the other hand, had different goals, that of self-improvement and character formation. Rosenstock (1921) likewise makes a clear distinction between adult and childhood education, stating that the difference is inherent in each group's life experiences and not in the content of the teaching material. According to Anderson and Lindeman, Rosenstock described the differences as follows: "Pedagogy is the method by which children are taught. Demagogy is the path by which adults are intellectually betrayed. Andragogy is the true method of adult learning" (1927, p. 2). Pöggeler (1999) points to other theorists who have concluded that the major task of andragogy is that of inspiring participants to self-fulfillment as individuals and thus the curricula and methods of adult educators must be different from those of childhood and youth teachers. Krajnc (1989) also makes a clear distinction between andragogy and pedagogy in her work, *Lifelong Education for Adults: An International Handbook*. Andragogy for Krajnc is concerned with the education of those who have not completed or who have interrupted their initial education so that they can take part in other major life activities. Pedagogy, on the other hand, is defined by the author as the primary or central educational activity in young people's lives.

Andragogy and research in Germany.

The general theme of research related to andragogy for the German educational philosophers centered on the development of workers' personalities in relation to the topics of culture and work. Some studies were also conducted in the area of adult education planning and management (Livecka, 1989). This work was performed predominantly by students working towards their Master of Arts degrees, through the main scientific-research institutes, such as the Academy of Pedagogic Sciences of the GDR, the Central Institute for Vocational Education and the Institute for Higher Education. This research created a firm basis for the GDR's training program and helped to establish a scientific system linked to the needs of both society and individuals (Savicevic, 1981). In the Federal Republic of Ger many the general theme of research since the 1970's has been the psychology of adult learning and curriculum development. While other countries have been involved in practice-oriented research, the FRG has taken the lead in discipline—oriented questions. The interest shown in research by the FRG has far out matched any other European country (Titmus, 1989).

Germany's involvement in research has also been sponsored by professional organizations. Reichmann (1999) has listed a few: (a) ISCAE—International Society for Comparative Adult Education, (b) ESREA—European Society for Research on the Education of Adults, (c) UNESCO—United Nations Educational, Scientific, and Cultural Organization, (d) Slovenian Institute for Adult Education.

ANDRAGOGY IN RUSSIA (1885)

The suppression of andragogy in Germany by Herbart did not stop the spread of this new concept into other countries. In the nineteenth century the concept of andragogy began to show up in Russian literature. The concept was first found used by Olesnicki, who was a professor at Kiev University in 1885. Olesnicki's familiarity with the German Literature introduced him to the concept of andragogy. His writings expressed the developmental concept of education, and the fact that it is realized within a person's period of development: childhood, youth, maturity and older age. It was held that one's education must be chosen in accordance with his or her state. Olesnicki believed optimistically regarding human development saying it can continue throughout life. Olesnicki upheld the concept that while physical strength may decline with age, the vigor of intellectual life in mature and even older people could be compared with the energy of youth. He held out a conceptual basis for andragogy explaining the importance of the developmental principle (Savicevic, 1989; 1991).

In the early years of the twentieth century, E. N. Medinski made attempts to set forth the theoretical foundations of andragogy by singling out andragogy as an independent sphere of scientific research. His concept of andragogy was that of andragogy having two parts, both andragogy and pedagogy. Even though Medin-ski's attempt was most interesting it did not meet wide support in the Soviet Union, as later the term "adult pedagogy" became popular. This was understood as a branch of pedagogy, and in some cases the term "extra curricular education" was used. This term developed by Medinski before the October revolution later became a part of the "peoples education." Later the term *anthropagogy*, meaning the science of teaching people, was composed. Medinski developed his thoughts in many works, but in particular the *Encyclopedia of Extra-Curricular Education*. Medinski was ahead of his time. He left behind a significant piece of work which contributed to the "establishment of adult education and learning as a scientific discipline." Savicevic believes this work is still in need of thorough investigation and proper assessment (Savicevic, 1991, p. 183; 1989).

Today the conception of andragogy in Russia is still rooted in adult-pedagogy which is still considered to be a part of pedagogy and is understood as the comprehensive science of education. In Russia adult pedagogy had been profoundly marked ideology. For many years Russian educators were reluctant to speak of andragogy because of political ideology: The concept of andragogy had developed in the opposite political ideological camp (Savicevic, 1991).

Among the prominent educational writers in Russia was A. Davineki. He regarded adult education as an integrated part of pedagogy which, above everything, reflected adult education, instruction and training. He held a very broad view of adult pedagogy and its scientific framework. Studies in adult pedagogy supersede that of children's education (Savicevic, 1991).

In the mid seventies N. K. Goncharov, the president of the Academy of Peda gogical Science, set forth his conception of andragogy. He saw andragogy as a synonym of adult pedagogy. In his 1976 work *Actual Problems of Pedagogy and Psychology of Adult Education*, Goncharov explained the development of andra-gogy elsewhere in the world and how it was being understood. He only wished Russia would give the concept of andragogy more consideration and he felt the development was too slow. Russian adult education eventually developed a series of sub-disciplines, believing that the theory of higher education is only a part of adult pedagogy. The subdisciplines are:

> Sociology of adult education psychology of growing old and pedagogical psychology of adults, adult didactics, instructional methods for individual subjects, night school pedagogy, production pedagogy, pedagogy of socio-cultural work, pedagogy of raising skills (Savicevic, 1991, p. 192).

Savicevic believes that Russia has broadened the framework of andragogy. He sees a problem in the conception which all these disciplines are assigned to as the category of pedagogy being the general science of education (1991).

In Russia, it is B. B. Ananev that has impacted andragogy the most in its move to becoming a science. Ananev relates that the theory of adult education did not until recently give the most approximate data on stages of maturity as it relates to people's lives. The important factors of the developmental stages and psycho-physical qualities have always been left out. Ananev and his associate's work became important to the constitution of andragogy in Russia. Savicevic sees this work as the provider for fresh information about intellectual development.

ANDRAGOGY IN POLAND (1900)

Andragogy also spread to Poland through Helen Radlinska, a Polish adult educator, along with others (Konewka, Kornilowiz, Godecki, Novicki, Bobrowski, Suchodalski), who developed varied aspects of adult education and adult learning. Radlinska, in her writings, used the term andragogy in place of the term "adult pedagogy." It was not until after World War II however, that Poland developed a specific concept of andragogy, which derived from the inter-war years and the existing tradition of this era. Adult educators followed the example of Radlinska and many of the Polish authors used andragogy in their writings, considering it a scientific discipline, focused on the study of all problems relating to adult education and learning. L. Turos also made a tremendous contribution to defining the concept of andragogy in Poland. He describes in detail the origins and evolution of andragogy, the research and methodological problems regarding andragogy, how andragogy is understood in the humanistic sciences, and the interrelatedness between andragogy and the other sciences as well as its scientific structure (Savicevic, 1991).

In Poland some educational writers stress the point that andragogy is not a question of "name alone". It is seen as a corresponding theory and methods which are much more complex and complicated than school pedagogy which uses a classroom system for teaching, and regular program of knowledge coupled with methods and sanctions to assure didactic (or self-learning) success. Savicevic, (1991) says Siemenski, a Polish adult educator, believes that andragogy is infanttilized when subjects and methods designed for children are transferred to the process of adult education and learning. Siemenski's view of the differences between andragogy and pedagogy is that they are different in categories.

> Everything is different, both the subject and object of education: Substance and methods; Institutions and means; Goals and possibilities; Family; Professional, social, and political tasks and functions (Savicevic, 1991, p.194).

Most Polish authors have agreed on a scientific structure underlying andragogy in a broad sense, accepting its methodological foundation, and have placed it among the humanistic sciences (Savicevic, 1991, p. 194).

Josef Polturzycki (1993), in answering to changes seen in adult education and the need for redefinition in Poland, states that some research in the field of psychology had advanced in the direction of looking for the differences in the educational needs and possibilities of youth and adults. Polturzycki says that so far the most important practical result is that observations of improved educational activities are being addressed regarding adult education. He observed that the more work done the more differences are clearly seen relating to the treatment of each section of education. Polturzycki says there must be complete autonomy for adult education: it must be seen as a separate educational system with its own aims, principles and participants. He also says it must have its own particular needs, interests and possibilities (1993).

Janusz Tymowski (1993), also a Polish adult educator, agrees with others in Poland who see the need to clearly distinguish between andragogy and pedagogy. Although Tymowski chooses to use the terminology of pedagogies for adults he says there is a difference between the two. He, like Siemenski, has categorized the two pedagogics saying:

Children accept teacher's word as the absolute truth which could not be questionable. Adults are learners with their own views of life, experiences, mastering definite spheres of work and life better than teachers do. Some times the knowledge acquired in the past is bad or even wrong, needing cer tain corrections. The focal point of learner-teacher communication in this case is the exchange of views (Tymowski, 1993, p.272).

Savicevic, (1991) suggested that Polish researchers and theoreticians of andragogy be willing to make a critical appraisal of the road they have come by, and then be willing to create a synthesis of their theoretical heritage. According to Savicevic, it does appear that this is the road Polish adult educators are taking.

ANDRAGOGY IN THE NETHERLANDS (1960)

Of all the countries practicing andragogy the Dutch concept is the most unique. Dutch andragogy was initiated in an attempt to meet the requirements of an exclusive and relatively independent movement for social workers and adult educators in the Netherlands. There was a great search among the academia of the Netherlands for a scientific and philosophical foundation for those in professional training of social workers and adult educators. These searchers were affected by many such philosophical foundations, one of which will receive special attention in this study. The theory of *sozialpädagogik*, which later translated into andragogy, originated in Germany and was elaborated by Paul Hetrop, an American. This gave Dutch andragogy a curious mixture of Anglo-American empiricism and German Idealism (van Gent, 1994).

The Dutch conception of andragogy.

The Dutch conception of andragogy has been classified by research as truly unique (Savicevic, 1991). This concept covers overall agogic work with adults, including their education. Ten Have broke down the German word *andragogik* into three distinct agogic divisions so as to scientifically cover the social and educational work with adults. *Andragogie* (andragogy), *andragogiek* (andragogic), and *andragologie* (andragology) were the divisions used by Ten Have. *Andragogie*, according to Ten Have, denotes the practice of the social and educational work done with adults. *Andragogiek* refers to a normative theory on the behalf of the art of social work and adult education and learning. Van Gent (1998) explains this to mean a sort of doctrine meant to serve as a guideline for practitioners, a specific layout of assumptions or statements on the nature of adults, with the best educational goals, the best didactic methods combined in a systematic manner. An example of this normative theory in the field of social work can be "casework" (1998). *Andragologie* is the science of social work and adult education and learning. A general notion of Dutch andragogy, as presented by Ten Have, would be that of anyone intentionally, in a professional way, conducting any activity designed to change the personality of another (Savicevic, 1991; van Gent, 1989).

Dutch andragogy as a scientific discipline.

Ten Have's andragology investigates both andragogy and andragogics from a scientific point of view. It is seen as the *logos* (Greek for *word*) of social work, the scientific analysis of andragogy just in the same way that psychology is the *logos* for the scientific study of the "psyche" (Savicevic, 1991; van Gent, 1998). Van Gent (1998) has observed that the distinctions between *andragologie* and *andragogick* has made it possible for Ten Have to combine, within the same conceptual framework, descriptive theories based on scientific research, as well as normative theories founded on philosophical conclusions (1998).

Andragogy became an accepted scientific discipline added to the school of study at the University of Amsterdam in 1966. By 1970, an amendment to the Academic Law authorized by the throne made every university in the Netherlands add andragogy to their program. The explanatory memorandum to each school made room for an explicit connection between "andragogy as a social science and the fields of social work, adult education, community organization, and personnel work" (Jarvis, 1992, p. 27). Dutch andragogy as a science draws upon the knowledge of other scientific disciplines such as psychology, sociology, and philosophy (Jarvis, 1992). Dutch andragogy is, therefore, considered multidisciplinary; it is not an autonomous science (van Gent, 1993).

Dutch andragogy and its relation to pedagogy.

The views held by researchers of Dutch andragogy vary where it concerns the relation between andragogy and pedagogy. Van Gent in his paper of 1984, "Andragogy in the Netherlands," presented at the Hungarian-Dutch Symposium, stated that "no sharp limit exists between pedagogic and andragogic work" (p. 10). He went on to explain that in a real situation there is usually a broad range of transitions, depending on the social variables. Van Gent holds that Ten Have did not concern himself greatly with the differences between the two but instead called attention to the similarities between the work of the pedagogues and the job of the andragogues (van Gent, 1984).

In response to the 1993 international survey published by the Slovenia Ministry of Science and Technology, three Dutch researchers answered to the question "What are your views on the relationship between adult education (andragogics) and education of children (pedagogics)?" (*Rethinking adult education for development*; Compendium, 1993, p. 29). In the following summary of the Dutch response, Kees Hammink (1993) views adult education theories and the theories of childhood education related but distinguishable, primarily by the subject being taught, and by the fact that the former deals with adults who seek to put their new learned knowledge immediately to work. Ad Boeren (1993) sees both andragogy and pedagogy to be distinctly different. He sees three major differences in all: 1) adult education is accomplished through voluntary acts; 2) adults come with experiences which can be used in the learning process; and 3) adults are willing to partake in adult education on the basis of specific personal need. The differences strongly influence the content, methodologies, organization, and management of the education system. Van Gent (1993) replies that both sciences are complementary and both sciences are interlinked. He explains the Dutch university system as having a department of andragology which forms together with several departments in the pedagogical field making a faculty of education. They share the same Bachelor of Arts (B.A.) curriculum but a different Master of Arts (M.A.) program. They become rivals only by competition for students and research grants.

Franz Pöggeler (1974) defined Dutch andragogy as being clearly distinguishable from pedagogy, which referred to child and youth education, the former referring to Gerontogogy, the theory of teaching elderly people. Pöggeler (1974) continues his explanation by stating that the difference between the two sciences should not be one of controversy or arguments, but one solely based on its facts.

ANDRAGOGY IN ENGLAND (1960'S)

Although the Adult Education Movement in England, according to Peers (1934), is one of the oldest organizations in mass education it accepted the concept of andragogy much later than other European countries and by way of America. Adult education as a system became an essential part of the struggle of the oppressed who used it to raise the level of the common life, it somehow assured them their right to share in the dignities and the advantages of a fuller citizenship. In the beginning adult education in England signified instruction in the elements of reading and writing for mature men and women who had been denied education opportunities as children. The universities before long became involved in offering education to the best adult students under the guidance of highly qualified university teachers.

Savicevic (1995) observes that the German understanding of andragogy did not penetrate the British thought regarding the education of adults in the early stage. However, the theory on adult education became an academic discipline in the 1920's. In this era, debates were strongly in favor of the possibility of teaching adults, and it was certain British authors who pointed out the characteristics of adult learning and education strongly criticizing the "theory of plasticity," which by this time had been enrooted in the concepts of British psychologists and pedagogues.

It was not until the early 1960's that J. A. Simpson brought attention to andragogy. In his writings Simpson pointed to the specific features of adult learning and education compared to that of children, demanding that the differences be made known. His interest concerned the finding of generalized methods applicable to all situations of adult learning and education instead of just techniques to be used with individual subjects (Savicevic, 1991).

By the end of the 1970's interest in andragogy in England began to spread, especially at the University of Nottingham. A special group was set up to examine the development of the andragogical theory. This group consisted of full-time and part-time Diploma in Adult Education students who encountered the term 'andragogy' while studying the topic *Adult Learning and Development*. The student group decided to examine the theories of Malcolm Knowles. They disagreed with Knowles' work which led them to look at Paulo Freire's work. Freire, a Brazilian adult educator, held a different view of adult education, a view preferred by the British students (The Nottingham Andragogy Group, 1983; Savicevic, 1991).

Several British writers took an interest in writing about andragogy, appreciating the fact that the conception of andragogy had a crucial impact on writings relating to problems of adult education and learning. While some authors opposed the term and conception others made attempts to lay conceptual foundations. Those accepting andragogy considered it to be a theory of adult education and learning, whereas those who do not see it as a special kind of ideology. English scholars continue to study the concept of andragogy in search of answering highlighted issues surrounding adult learners (Savicevic, 1991; Challis, 1996).

Andragogy in Europe today.

Today andragogy has spread across many countries and is interpreted differently depending on the country. However, the general concept of andragogy in European countries is derived from the intended meaning developed in Germany, which is, the science that seeks to understand the adult's learning habits through out the adult's life. This science also studies the educational practices of the adult educator in formal or non-formal ways. Andragogy studies the history of adult education along with the philosophies of education and any other sciences that affect the educational development of the adult. Andragogy is considered scientific because of its long historical development which has been documented and is traceable to its inception in 1833. Andragogy has linked itself to many relevant sciences (Boyd & Apps, 1984; Savicevic, 1995) which have offered empirical data relating to the cognitive development of the adult's intelligence and learning habits. It has sought in the past to treat the concerns of the adult socially, economically, psychologically, spiritually, biologically, physiologically, ethically and gerontologically (Savicevic, 1995). Andragogy in Europe is understood as an independent discipline. It has developmental stages and experiences similar to other established sciences. It is seen worthy as a university subject and as a research field; offering a mass of knowledge pertaining to the adult learner.

Because it is accepted as a scientific discipline in Europe, there are many inter national organizations that recognize its practice. Thus these organizations and institutions offer controlling qualities, training, certification, opportunities for research and recognition of scientific accomplishments in the field.

Through the years andragogy in Europe has proved its capability to create its own theoretical constructs, through access to research data, tools and organizations. This creation has provided results that are usable by other sciences. In Europe the linking of andragogy with other disciplines, which has already resulted in empirical research, has provided additional strength and credence, and andragogy has given them a wealth of data regarding adult learning and education.

ANDRAGOGY IN AMERICA (1926)

American andragogy started with Lindeman (1926) who imported the term and intended for it to serve the same purpose it did in Germany. However, with a lapse of almost forty-five years between the initial introduction of the concept and its gaining public recognition, American andragogy took on a meaning of its own.

THE INTRODUCTION OF ANDRAGOGY TO THE U.S.

Edward Lindeman (1885–1953) is considered to be the father of modern adult education, the spiritual father of American andragogy, and the "creator of the framework for discourse and analysis predominant in adult education" (Brook field, 1984, p. 185; Davenport & Davenport, 1984, 1986; Nixon-Ponder, 1995; Stewart, 1987). Lindeman's work in the field of adult education involved the writing of books, articles, public presentations, service in the university system as a professor of social work as well as in the church as an associate pastor (Brook field, 1987; Davenport & Davenport, 1986).

In 1926, Lindeman and Martha Anderson visited Germany in order to study educational experiences. While there they examined the German Folk High School system and the educational institution of the worker's movement. As a result of their comparative research, Lindeman and Anderson discovered the German concept of andragogy as used at the Academy of Labor Frankfurt-am-Main. The concept and its term were later transferred to America in an interpretative translation of literature from the Academy of Labor (Brookfield, 1987; Davenport & Davenport, 1986; Savicevic, 1995). Anderson and Lindeman's (1927) work, *Education Through Experience*, communicates the concept of andragogy as understood by Eugene Rosenstock and the staff at the Academy of Labor. Their research describes the activities of the Academy, its philosophy, its course schedules and its definition of andragogy as the "true method of adult learning" (p. 2). Anderson and Lindeman further state that, "In andragogy, theory becomes fact; that is, words become responsible acts, accountable deeds, and the practical fact which arises out of necessity is illumined by theory..." (p. 2–3). The writers make a clear distinction between child and adult education. "Adult and child education", they say, "can no longer be distinguished by materials, content: literature for children and politics for men. The distinction is inherent in life itself: between the child and the adult lies the field of action" (p. 3). Anderson and Lindeman saw this distinction in an adult's life as being one of experience and history, things that are foreign to a child. Children's education is perceived as working in accordance with nature while adult education conflicts with nature.

Anderson and Lindeman (1927) proceeded to explain adult experience as a life filled with social interaction and personal striving; as a result, the adult learner brings to the classroom a "world of unarranged and untested conceptions, terms, and elements of education" (p. 4). Andragogy was thus seen as experience related.

Anderson and Lindeman never made any serious attempt to develop the ideas they introduced to American literature. Prior to the publication of their book, Lindeman published a brief article in the Workers' Education Journal in an effort to introduce the concept of andragogy (Davenport & Davenport, 1984). The following is the very first known record of the use of andragogy in America:

> Professor Eugene Rosenstock of the Frankfurt Academy of Labor has coined a new word: andragogik. He distinguishes between pedagogy, which is the method for miseducating adults; and *andragogy [emphasis added]*, which is the true method by which adults keep themselves intelligent about the modern world. Andragogik represents the learning process according to which theoretical knowledge and practical affairs become resolved in creative experience. The word, andragogik, is perhaps a bit awkward, a bit artificial but the meaning behind it is significant for those who would be either learners or teachers. Workers' education will make a qualitative difference in the life of our time only if it discovers a learning method which is more dynamic than that of conventional education. (Stewart, 1987, p. 109)

Marius Hansome (1931), a doctoral student at Columbia University, also spoke of andragogy in his dissertation, *World Workers' Educational Movements: Their Social Significance*. In it he describes journeys to Europe and attendance at many international workers' union meetings. Like Anderson and Lindeman, Hansome makes reference to the Academy of Labor Frankfurt am-Main Germany. Hansome reports on the involvement of Dr. Eugene Rosenstock, the first principal of the Academy. Rosenstock found the methods of pedagogy inadequate for adults. This, Hansome says, led to the use of a new theory of teaching known as andragogy, which he summarized in the following three propositions:

1. The adult worker is in possession of a considerable store of ideas, experiences, concepts, general knowledge, misinformation, an accumulation that is more or less chaotic, uncoordinated, more or less unverified, but held with some tenacity because it is overlaid with feeling and a tone grown out of struggle and pain. He has also observed a discrepancy between principle and practice which adds to his confusion and sickening heart.

2. The adult worker's mind operates best in an atmosphere of controversy. Conflict of ideas keeps him alert. Therefore, debate, criticism, discussion and opposition are forms through which he can learn.

3. The adult worker cannot assimilate, cannot harbor new ideas and information unless at the same time he eliminates the old, untenable ideas and cherished notions. He learns best through a living interchange of the substance of thought (Hansome, 1931, p. 183–184).

This concept of andragogy was also of interest to Wayne Pirtle (1966), a doctoral student of the University of California, Berkeley, who wrote his dissertation on *The History of Adult Education in Germany 1800–1933*. His work extensively covered the era of the German Folk high schools including the *Die Akademie der Arbeit* (The Academy of Labor in Frankfurt-am-Main). Pirtle, like Lindeman, Anderson and Handsome, gives Dr. Eugene Rosenstock the credit for the success of the Academy and the use of the term *andragogik*. Pirtle regarded the Academy as an innovation in adult education because of the effort of the University of Frankfurt to establish a college for workers without formal academic preparation. Pirtle (1966) refers to Rosenstock with great respect, pointing out his role in "interesting government circles in a work-education program for the unemployed" (p. 333). Pirtle, like his American predecessors, made no attempt to develop a theory or a philosophy on andragogy but used his historical work as a body of knowledge that added to the field of adult education in America (1966).

The most recognized author and educator in the field of adult learning in the U.S. is Malcolm Knowles (1913–1997), known as the major proponent of andragogy in America. Knowles first became an adult educator in 1935 (Jarvis, 1987), immediately after his graduation from Harvard University (Carlson, 1989). He regarded Lindeman as his mentor, and referenced him many times in his book, *The Meaning of Adult Education* (1926). For Knowles, however, it was not until 1966 (Sopher, 2003) that he was introduced to the term andragogy by Dusan Savicevic, a Yugoslavian adult educator (Carlson, 1989; Knowles, 1990; Savice vic, 1995).

Knowles' first published work on andragogy was "Andragogy, not Pedagogy," published in *Adult Leadership* (1968), but it was his book, *The Modern Practice of Adult Education: Andragogy versus Pedagogy, (1970)*, that became his most noteworthy. This work, according to Peter Jarvis (1987), "set out to be a complete practical guide for the adult educator and as such it covered all the ground that he considered should be examined by adult educators" (p. 175). Knowles used his book to introduce his understanding of the difference between andragogy and pedagogy, presenting them as opposing fields of education. Jarvis felt that the crude distinction of the two was the spark that set off a debate in adult education circles that lasted into the 1980's; and that this debate is similar to those of the nineteenth century when the term was first introduced.

Knowles' (1973) book, *The Adult Learner: A Neglected Species*, was written in order to install andragogy as a teaching theory in adult learning. Knowles authored a total of 19 books (Henschke, 1997/1998), two of which were later to be considered seminal books (Jarvis, 1987): The revised editions of *The Modern Practice of Adult Education*, with the sub-title *From Pedagogy to Andragogy*; and *Andragogy in Action*.

Knowles' (1980) theory of andragogy can be found in his assumptions regarding andragogy and his andragogical model. This "andragogical model," says Knowles:

> …is not an ideology; it is a system of alternative sets of assumptions. And this leads us to the critical difference between the two models. The pedagogical model is an ideological model which excludes the andragogical assumptions. The andragogical model is a system of assumptions which includes the pedagogical assumptions. (1990, p. 64)

Knowles (1990) explains that the assumptions are to be used at the teacher's discretion, depending on the need of the student. If a situation calls for pedagogical assumptions, they should be used, and if it calls for andragogical assump tions, those should be used.

In summarizing Knowles' views on andragogy, Weingand (1996) calls Knowles' assumptions "cornerstones upon which the concept of andragogy itself is built" (p.79).

The American concept of andragogy.

The American concept of andragogy has been built upon the tenets of Malcolm Knowles (1990), who claims that it took him over ten years to formulate his the ory of adult learning. Knowles explains that his earliest construction of the andragogical model of education was the antithesis of the existing pedagogical model (1990).

Knowles (1990) admits that in his book, *The Modern Practice of Adult Education: Andragogy Versus Pedagogy* (1970), he is stating his model of pedagogy and that of andragogy are antithetical; that pedagogy is bad for adults and andragogy is better, that pedagogy is for children and andragogy is developed for adults. However, after meeting with several school teachers who claimed that andragogical methods worked for them, as well as trainers and teachers of adults who declared the andragogical model did not always work, he changed his position. In the revision, *The Modern Practice of Adult Education: From Pedagogy to Andragogy* (1980), Knowles declares his new position on andragogy. He asserts that pedagogy is an ideology and that andragogy is a system of alternative assumptions. Knowles says that educators can use either the pedagogical model or the andragogical model, depending on which is most realistic in a given situation.

The American andragogical concept also concerns itself with how adults should be educated (Knox, 1991), thus making it a method or a teaching technique (Nottingham Andragogy Group, 1983). Knowles' adult education is prescriptive in nature, meaning Knowles issues directives as to how a teacher should conduct his/her self in the process of educating the adult learner (Knox, 1991; Savicevic, 1995 Elias, 1980; Hartree, 1984).

The concepts of andragogy in the U.S. are firmly rooted in Knowles' teaching theory. However, in the 1980's, two other schools of thought regarding andragogy were crystallized. The first denied both andragogy and pedagogy, urging that a general science regarding education and learning be developed. This concept is known as humanology. The second school of thought urged a separate scientific discipline designed to study education and the learning of adults, but lacked a particular name by which it could be called (Savicevic, 1995).

For some American authors, understanding andragogy became a matter of semantics, so other terms seen as more appropriate were coined. Lebel (1978) wrote on the need for a concept he called "gerogogy," which entailed the learning of older adults. Knudsen (cited by Hartree, 1984) seeks to promote the concept of "humanology," a combination of pedagogy, andragogy, and gerogogy. Yeo (1982) preferred the development of the concept "eldergogy," which deals with the education of the elderly.

The difference between Pedagogy and Andragogy in the U.S.

Knowles (1990) implies that the difference between pedagogy and andragogy has to do more with the teacher than it does with the student, or for that matter theory. He says:

The pedagog, perceiving the pedagogical assumptions to be the only realistic assumptions, will insist that the learners remain dependent on the teacher; whereas the andragog, perceiving that movement toward the andragogical assumptions is a desirable goal, will do everything possible to help the learners take increasing responsibility for their own learning (p. 64).

Adult educators across the U.S. have varied in their conclusions regarding the differences between andragogy and pedagogy and how they are related. Cervero (1993) sees andragogy and pedagogy in the U.S. as interlinked, yet they are rivals. By this he means that the philosophy of education has too narrowly focused on the schooling of children and that there should be more attention placed on the continuities in education rather than the differences in education. His contemporary, Charters (1993), thinks the principles of education are the same for children and adults, though adults have different ranges of experience, goals, and education. At the same time it does not seem right, says Charters, to have two discrete classes, andragogy and pedagogy. Houle (1993) conversely feels that American andragogy is appropriate for children as well as adults. The question of the precise relationship between andragogy and pedagogy is still undecided by many U.S. educators.

10

DIFFERENCES OF THE ADULT LEARNER

As we age our brain changes, creating distinct neurological differences between the child and the adult. The former possesses an underdeveloped brain and the latter a matured or developed brain. This occurs through brain growth and weight by a process known as "complexity", which is the growth of neurons as they divide and spread, and also by a process referred to earlier as myelination—cells forming a fatty tissue which wraps around the nerve conduit like an insulation, this growth and development occurs anatomically, changing not only the weight of the brain but also the size—at this stage the adult brain has a GI of 2.6 in healthy respondents.

This growth and size resulting into a matured brain is, in turn, outwardly measured by acts of maturity and the ability to plan in advance and control one's behavior. This ability is attributed to the development of the frontal lobes, which is a process that begins at birth and continues for approximately twenty years. The developed brain's increase in neurons will result in a total of 1,000 trillion by this time. This is the work of complexity but it is not automatic nor a function of time. It happens in response to experiences in enriched learning environments (Hart, 1999). Carter (1998) observed that the full mediation of the frontal lobes of the developed brain causes the decision making process to become less emotional and impulsive. This, she says, happens only at full adulthood.

DIFFERENCE IN AGE

The best way to differentiate the child and the adult, for educational purposes, may be by explaining the development of the brain. If the biological differences of the development of the human brain can be categorized by a chronological age, then an age for adulthood can be set. Many neuroscientists have mentioned developmental characteristics of the brain that make it possible to pin down some specifics of brain development and ages. These differences mark a clear distinction between children and adults although the literature on human development varies in definition regarding chronological sequences of adult developmental stages.

Bloom, Beal, and Kupfer (2003) agree on age twenty as a reasonable chronological age at which to set brain development and the true beginning of adulthood. They say it takes that long for the brain to self-construct and that the period between the early twenties through the fifties is considered the prime of life.

Bloom and company have placed this development of the brain in three progressive stages. First, they state that the child's brain spends time wiring up. Second, they say the adolescent's brain spends time developing the frontal lobe. Third and last, the adult brain is concerned with plasticity. It is at this stage that the brain is now truly ready to form new habits, adjust to new circumstances, and learn new ways. The adult brain begins early to rely on plasticity because it is needed for memory which, in the healthy adult, becomes a lifelong resource and at some point supports virtually all of the cognitive abilities. It is at twenty that the brain begins to send signal transmission throughout the entire central nervous system.

The evidence accumulated on brain development seems to strongly suggest that full adulthood is not attained until twenty and in some cases not until the early twenties.

Monte Buchsbaum, director of the Neuroscience PET Laboratory at Mount Sinai School of Medicine, also infers that brain development is complete in the twenties. He makes this inference from research conducted on fifty normal volunteers ranging in ages from twenty to eighty-seven. Buchsbaum scanned the brains of each of his volunteers and concluded that he did not detect significant differences in brain development between the twenty-five year old brains and the eighty-seven year old brains.

Dr. Kathlie Nunley (2003), educational psychologist, writes on the challenges faced by the adult brain when confronted by the youth's brain or the child's brain. She points out that maturity plays a big role because it takes about twenty years to fully develop the pre-frontal cortex, making it difficult for the teen to control impulsive behaviors. Thus, adolescents unlike adults have problems quickly sizing up the risks in life as well as making good long-term decisions; and there is some evidence that points to longer development for some regions of the brain. Kurt Fischer and Samuel Rose (1998) relate the research in cognitive neuroscience to a growth cycle that repeats itself several times between the time of birth and thirty years of age; while previous development was seen as a sequence of stages it is now understood as recurring growth cycles where both behavior and the brain experience change in repeating patterns.

DIFFERENCE IN BRAIN DEVELOPMENT

When charting the changes adults go through as they grow older, it is tempting to classify them in a negative way, and to see aging as debilitating. This book deals with the facts of aging, but views them in a positive way, showing much optimisim for adults as they go through the aging process, thus the changes listed are referred to as a graduation process (See Table 1 in Chapter XI).

THE GRADUATION PROCESS

Loss of neurons.

By the early twenties the brain has increased its mass of neurons from 100 billion to three fold. It was once taught that as many as 100,000 of these neurons were lost a day. However, new research shows that this may not be the case, but rather, individual rates of brain cell loss vary a great deal. When these cells are lost it is believed to be mostly in the frontal and temporal cortex, and especially the motor cortex. Neurons, dendrites and synapses are all lost as a result of aging. The brain begins to lose its original thickness and variations of thickness. At this point the difference between youths and adults become obvious. The cortex shrinks when the surface becomes more atrophic like any other muscle in the body as a result of aging (Howard, 2000; Andreasen, 2001).

Weight loss.

As a result of the loss of, and shrunken, neurons the brain size declines from a mean value of approximately 4.0mm in youth to 3.12mm in an eighty-two year old adult. Brain weight loss averages 10% in the average healthy person's lifetime (See Fig. 18). In men, this loss is more obvious than in women. Men lose more weight in the left hemisphere which controls language. Women will experience about a two-ounce drop in brain mass around the time of menopause, while men on the other hand experience accelerated loss at around sixty years of age (Howard, 2000; Andreasen, 2001). When these changes begin, the adult brain begins to be very different; while some adults' brains age gracefully, others decline considerably. The loss of weight and volume however is just a small percentage of the grand total. Also, this loss does not affect the remaining neurons which are still able to change their synaptic connections, in turn, providing for lifelong learning (Marieb, 1999; Andreasen, 2001).

Cognitive decline.

Aging is accompanied by some cognitive decline in areas such as spatial ability, speed of perception, decision making, reaction time and memory, these result because of areas affected by age, as demonstrated in Fig. 19. However, all adults do not experience decline at the same rate. The healthy adult has the ability to build on their experiences, mathematical skills and verbal fluency. Cattell (1967), Horn (1970) and more recently Marieb (1999), are in agreement that while certain cognitive abilities decline in the aging adult, others do not. As stated earlier Cattell and Horn referred to those that decline as fluid intelligence and those that do not as crystallized. While Restak (2001) holds that certain cognitive skills like grammar and vocabulary do not necessarily decline over time, it is just that some people lack the ability to recall information rapidly.

In the past such decline was considered senility, but Marieb (1999) writes that only five percent of older people demonstrate true senility. Heidemann (2003) reported that approximately two-thirds of Americans age sixty and older experience a significant decline in cognitive abilities including memory, concentration, clarity of thought, focus and judgement. However, one-third of this age group do not experience significant decline in cognitive reasoning. Heidemann concludes that instead of the brain inevitably deteriorating as formerly believed, the aging brain can maintain itself and operate efficiently into extremely old age.

Shift of brain use.

As adults age the region of the brain responsible for working memory begins to also age. When Restak (2001) compared the prefrontal cortices of a child at nine to an adult at twenty-four, he found that the FMRI showed activation of a child to be greater. Restak explains that this suggests children will use more of the prefrontal area for the task of remembering important information. The adult learner, on the other hand, proves to be more efficient, by using the smaller area

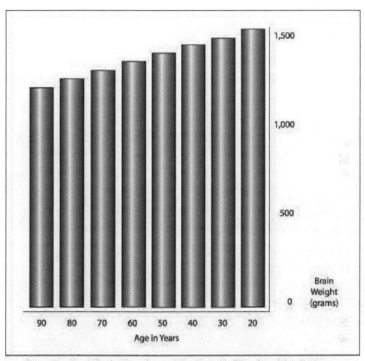

**Learning is affected by loss of brain weight and cell isolation.
After the ages of 40 and 50 years the adult brain loses about
2% of its overall weight every decade.**

Figure 18 Brain weight loss scale

Areas affected by age, each affected at different rates.

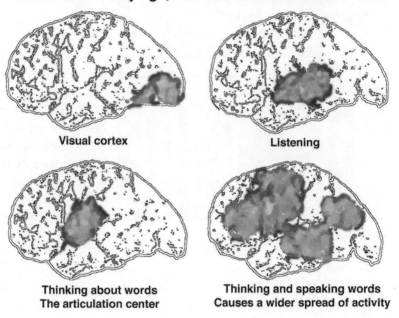

Visual cortex

Listening

Thinking about words
The articulation center

Thinking and speaking words
Causes a wider spread of activity

Figure 19 Areas affected by age at different rates

of the brain. This Restak believes is "due to molecular and cellular changes that occur during the years of development" (p. 81). Restak concludes that even when youth and older persons perform equally well on a task, the brain of the young person will go about doing the task in a different way, and vice versa.

A study reported by Dr. K. S. Knalsa (in Heidemann, 2003) agrees with Restak's findings. Twenty-five to thirty percent of the eighty year olds tested were able to score just as high on tests of cognitive functioning as were the group of young people. Dr. Knalsa reported that some of those in their 80's and 90's performed even better than the majority of the youngsters.

Change in blood flow.

Another characteristic of the adult brain is the change in blood flow. Andreasen (2001) points out that the general decline in cortical thickness at about age fifty is related to blood flow. She says that the aging brain maintains more or less the same level of general metabolic activity as aging occurs. It has also been observed that the aging brain has fewer nerve cells in some regions because of the minimal blood flow to some brain regions. An example of this is the low blood flow in the visual cortex, leading to the need for reading glasses. Another example is the decrease of blood flow to the cingulated region, which is the part of the brain that is important for alertness and arousal.

Andreasen (2001) sees a positive correlation in some cases, in the healthy adult, with some regions of the brain. Increased blood flow occurs if there is a region with nerve cell failure occurring. The increased blood flow to these regions helps the remaining cells work harder at survival. Andreasen uses the hippocampus as an example because this is usually the first region affected by Alzheimer's disease,(See Fig. 20 & 21 for regions of the brain affected by Alzheimer's). Blood flow changes are noted when there is a recognized change in the functional capacities. Andreasen believes that blood flow changes can be experienced in some people as early as the late forties and early fifties. The older the brain gets, the more diffuse the changes become (2001).

These changes in the development of the adult brain are responsible for the individual diversity. Both neuroscientists and educators attest to these differences. It is now agreed on that a class of fourth graders will be at the same stage socially, physically, mentally, and be capable of certain learning tasks, with limited life experiences. An adult class on the other hand may consist of students ranging from eighteen to eighty, and will all be at different levels socially, physically and mentally. Research also shows that the older the learner gets the more

The left side displays a healthy brain, while the right side displays a brain affected by Alzheimer's disease showing skrinkage.

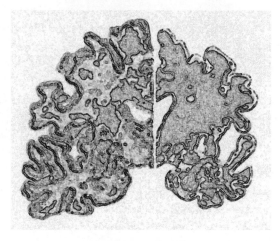

Figure 20 Brain affected by Alzheimer's disease

This is the MRI of a healthy brain

This is the MRI of a brain
affected by Alzheimer's.
This area stores personal memories.

This is the MRI of a brain
affected by semantic dementia.
Here people tend to forget
general things.

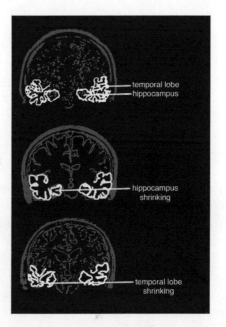

temporal lobe
hippocampus

hippocampus
shrinking

temporal lobe
shrinking

Figure 21 Drawings of MRIs of healthy and affected brains

diversified he/she becomes. Examples of this are the dissimilarities of forty-four year-olds compared to the similarities of a group of twenty-year-olds (Restak, 2001; D'Arcangelo, 2000; Darkenwald & Merriam, 1982).

Age and memory.

Bloom, Geal, and Kupfer (2003) in the *DANA Guide to Brain Health*, inform us that no one will recall a story or commit a name to memory in the same way at age seventy-six as we were able to do at age sixteen, simply because the mental context in which we perform these functions may have changed over the years. However, most of what has been stored in our minds throughout life remains there; it is not lost. What excessively becomes noticeable after time is the ease or speed with which one is able to retrieve things from memory. Retrieving memories slows with time. Bloom, et al., believes that this slowing down of memory begins as early as age twenty, even before one begins to anticipate age-related changes in brain activity. Signal transmission throughout the entire central nervous system begins to slow a little over time. It is not much, maybe just a few milliseconds each year, continuing throughout adulthood.

Bloom, et al. (2003) have pointed out that this memory loss is a part of the natural aging process which takes many, many years and becomes noticeable in everyday perceptions or movements. Not all memories are affected in the same way. Tasks that are constantly repeated and involve both physical and mental exertion are less vulnerable to age related slowdown, such as playing a musical instrument. Memory for language is generally well preserved, but the processing of rapid speech creates a problem. Bloom, et al. agree that everyone has a lapse of memory now and then, but as we all get older we begin to worry more and more about such lapses. As they get older many people reaching mid-life begin to fear they may completely lose their memory. However, research today proves this is not the case. It has now been established that the healthy adult's brain does not have to suffer a major loss of memory at any age. The effects of age on memory were discussed at length in earlier chapters.

11

NEUROANDRAGOGY AND NEW THEORETICAL PERSPECTIVES ON ADULT LEARNING AND ADULT EDUCATION

Linking the scientific data regarding the adult brain and its cognitive functions with practice in the field of andragogy results in a move in a new direction. This chapter moves from the analytical to the synthetic. Here further practical links with theory, facts and practice are made. In keeping with the topic and aim of this writing a few issues affecting the concept of andragogy will be examined and the research applied: the perspectives of adult learning theories, the perspectives of the adult learner, and the perspectives of adult intelligence. This is not intended to be an exhaustive list of issues, neither are any of these issues discussed entirely. This list is only a starting point in the neuroandragogical approach to the analysis of a series of important questions presently existing in modern andragogy.

NEW RESEARCH LEADS TO NEW MEASURES

The adult brain has come to be regarded as a highly complex and uniquely developed constructed functional system which is now understood in new terms and defined with new principles. The education and training of adult students can no longer be guided by principles driven by old myths and antiquated research. With new knowledge about such a sophisticated instrument as the brain we must begin to draw up new principles, new theories, and new methods that will reflect the true activity of the adult brain.

FORMER PERSPECTIVES ON ADULT LEARNING THEORIES

The former perceptions of adult learning are derived from controlled tests on animals, children and in some cases adults. Most conclusions on learning make no distinction between children and adults, and applications are in most cases applicable to both groups. Researchers in andragogy have used the research provided by psychologists for almost a hundred years as a scientific foundation to support its theories and practice in adult education. In doing this they have chosen to overlook the fact that the science it has chosen to align with has always been more concerned with children than it has with adults. Research accomplished by associationists, behaviorists, Gestalt psychologists and cognitive theorists, must now be re-evaluated for relevance in the creating of current perceptions of adult learning.

Darkenwald and Merriam (1982) have noted that there are so many approaches and views presented by psychologists that neither the behaviorists, the Gestaltists, nor the cognitive theorists are able to agree on what constitutes adult learning in conjunction with aging. The only thing agreed on, says Darkenwald and Merrian, is the view of learning being a phenomenon which is evidenced by a change in behavior. The following are the learning perceptions held by the leading psychologists:

1. Thorndike, an associationist, developed the theory of "connectionism" or what is also known as the "S-R." He taught that learning is a process of association. He explains that the receiving of stimulus is followed by the connection of something familiar; a bond is then made. He deplored repetition as learning in that there are no connections being made. Most behaviorists seek to follow Thorndike, explaining learning in terms of a connection between physical stimuli and responses that are observable.

2. B. F. Skinner, a behaviorist, explains learning as happening out of the reinforcement of a connection made between stimulus and response. As a result all behavior is learned and can be modified if certain environmental factors are put in place in a predetermined manner. Most behaviorists seek to follow

Skinner, explaining learning in terms of a connection between physical stimuli and responses that are observable.

3. The Gestaltists disagree with the definition given by the behaviorists who are accused of depending too much on the nervous system. They suggested examining the whole, not just individual parts. Gestaltists believe learning must be seen as a total structure not just isolated incidents. They gained a strong hold on the field of education and greatly impacted the field with their learning theory. They believe:

    - Learning cannot be determined by studying a stimulus.

    - The perception of the environment cannot be an isolated experience.

    - Learning must include the investigation of the notions of understanding, insight, and the solving of problems.

Jean Piaget, a well known cognitive psychologist, did most of his work with children and made a great impression on the field of education in general. He, like other cognitive psychologists, focused on the mental processes; thinking, concept-formation and how knowledge is acquired. Jerome Bruner, Ausubel, and Robert Gagne, all cognitive psychologists, made an effort to define learning in an age related manner. They decried rote memory and promoted that learning had meaning instead. They also spoke of discovery learning. This they say happens outside of given content which must be discovered and then internalized. There is also the explanation that learning is a result of a controlled environment that can be manipulated and studied. Learning must therefore be seen as observable change.

Cross (1981) views adult learning perceptions in four additional ways. First, she states that learning psychology offers the definition of learning as the measurement of mental ability, perception, memory, forgetting and other cognitive functions. She states that unfortunately psychologists interest in adult learning narrows down to the measuring of intelligence. Some psychologists, she claims, are looking at the psychological aging of cells and how this may affect the sensory functions of vision, hearing, and reaction of time. A second source of information on adults as learners comes from research on adult development. Here Cross says we gain a broad and ill-defined category that includes such things as; research on life cycles, ego and personality, cognitive and intellectual development. The other two forms mentioned by Cross are self-directed learning and organized instruction.

There is certainly plenty of evidence that psychologists have tried to offer approaches to human learning with some relevance to education and the under standing of adults as learners. However, these perceptions pose problems for adult education for different reasons. First, none of the psychologists have the same opinion on learning theories so their conclusions are different. Second, the conclusions made are so general that they can fit adult or child. Third, they have not provided any distinct definition for the child nor for the adult, therefore, it is difficult to differentiate adult learning from childhood learning.

If andragogy is to attain learning perceptions that are more specific, it must now turn its attention to research that emphasizes learning as a cognitive function of aging. Only by doing this will adult learning be "differentiated in a hierarchical sense" (Darkenwald and Merriam, 1984, p.104)

Neuroandragogy uses the findings that relate specifically to the learning pro cess, bearing in mind the unique qualities of adulthood including the developed brain. This creates a clear distinction between the definition of learning for adults and children.

NEW PERSPECTIVES ON ADULT LEARNING THEORIES

Andragogy is guided by assumptions of adult learning that seek to define the unique qualities of the adult as learner. So far, the learning definitions or explanations used by andragogy have failed to make a clear distinction. Darkenwald and Merriam (1982) claim that a distinction will only be made when we understand the unique qualities of adulthood as they relate to the learning process. Neuroandragogy offers new directions in the viewing of adult learning and its uniqueness. It sees the differences between the learning and education of the child and that of the adult, necessitating a different approach when working with adult students.

Outside of studies in neuroscience and biology, it is difficult to find a definition of learning that accentuates the neurophysiological functions, or a definition that shows a distinct difference between adult and child.

To begin with, all learning is a complex biological process which depends on synaptic plasticity. This includes the action of neurotransmitters and postsynaptic receptors, figure 5 and figure 10 in chapter two demonstrate the activity of the cells in the brain when learning occurs. However, it is now very clear to scientists that the learning of adults is very different at the cognitive level. Therefore this indicates the need to define adult learning in different terms.

In order to do so, a few observations of the learning habits of the brain must first be observed: In any learning activity the brain is storing information and at a later time retrieves it. In order to do this, synaptic plasticity must be possible. This action depends on a complex biochemical process which involves neurotransmitters and receptors. It is also believed that the information is first stored in chunks throughout the brain then reconstructed at a later time for the purpose of recall. This may be what some researchers call the filing of information. This action of learning is performed in unique ways in the adult brain. Andreasen (2001) states that the functions are different because the adult brain is more mature. The following are differences in the action of the adult brain during learning activities:

1. The adult's learning occurs at a higher optimal level, caused by special brain receptors (Salem, as cited in Bass, 1994).

2. Adult experiences affect the development of perceptual and cognitive abilities through the reorganization of brain structure. The adult experiences contribute to higher level reasoning (Elbert, Heim & Rockstrah, 2001; Fisher & Rose, 1998).

3. Adults process information slower than their young counterparts because of care to make fewer errors. Reconstruction and retrieval is slow and new information searches carefully for stored information to make connections (Restak, 2001), which modifies connections between nerve cells.

4. Adults rely less on the emotional centers of the limbic system for decision-making and reasoning. The reasoning of the adult is therefore more rational (Carter, 1998).

5. The adult economizes on the use of the brain for processing new information. While the youth utilizes the neurocortex to a great extent, the adult will use the hippocampus for storing the information, then the cortex for recall (Restak, 2001; Carter, 1998).

Adult learning defined.

Bearing these facts in mind, neuroandragogy defines adult learning as: The most relevant information passing through the cortex to the hippocampus where it is then stored. If this information finds other stored information in the brain, it connects, if not, it begins to make new memory. If used shortly after, this memory becomes permanent in the hippocampus and is pulled up by the cortex at the time of recall. If used daily or frequently enough information may remain in the cortex for quick references. This is all made possible by a complex chemical interaction being performed at a high optimal level, releasing transmitters by special post and pre-synaptic receptors. In turn new synaptic connections are formed. The retrieval of the stored information is sometimes a slow process, performed by the neurocortex. If pressured the recall is even slower or can be delayed for days.

FORMER PERSPECTIVES ON THE ADULT LEARNER

It is extremely important to andragogy that the differences between adults and children are made clear because of the profound implications for education. Andragogy has always seen the need to understand adulthood in connection with how adults learn to better facilitate the learning experience.

Alexander Kapp tried to highlight this fact when he coined the term andragogy coming from the Greek derivative *adros* meaning "adult." Kapp saw the importance of adults being recognized as adults, and the fact that they are different they should be taught differently. Rosenstock also saw the need to differentiate adult students because their lives are different, so are their ideas, their experiences, concepts and wrong information. Also, Rosenstock concluded that the adult student's mind operates best in an atmosphere of differences and opposing views. Knowles was no different from his German predecessors in the field of andragogy. He too saw the need to distinguish between the adult differences and the child when it comes to learning.

Knowles' distinction between both as it relates to learning may be the most popular among adragologists. In his book *The Modern Practice of Adult Education* (1980), he sees the adult as one who moves from dependency towards self-direction, as one who has accumulated a growing reservoir of experiences and established self-identity. Knowles also says that the readiness of adults to learn distinguishes them from children and has some connection to the developmental tasks of their social role. He sees the adult as more problem-centered than subject-centered when it comes to learning.

However, to say independence declares adulthood poses a problem in today's world where children are being left to fend for themselves at a very early age. Also the notion of experience being a sign of adulthood is a contemporary problem, because forced independence creates problems and frightening experiences of its own. The third assumption put fourth by Knowles regarding a readiness to learn can be a feature among children also who want to learn video games and computer skills at a very early age.

Darkenwald and Merriam (1982) are of the opinion that in our society it is independence that determines adulthood more than any other factor. Society has dubbed those who have assumed responsibilities as being adults. Very few researchers are willing to use age as an indicator for adulthood. In society chronological age does not provide a reliable indicator for making a demarcation between children and adults, according to Darkenwald and Merriam.

However, Johnstone and Rivera (in Darkenwald and Merriam, 1982, p.77) in their study on adulthood and adult education listed chronological age as an important indicator for adulthood along with being married and the head of a household. Many uncertainties still remain when we begin to define the characteristics of an adult for the purpose of adult education.

NEW PERSPECTIVES ON THE ADULT LEARNER

Neuroandragogy sees the most reliable description of adulthood to be chronological age. This is in agreement with Johnstone's and Revera's research on adults and adult education. Those who use age as an indicator for adulthood vary in their conclusions. For the sake of psychological testing, the age is set at sixteen. Also, Roger Gould's (1978) adult developmental stage begins at sixteen. Those involved in adult education seem to prefer eighteen as the recognizable age for adulthood. Savicevic (1988), has used eighteen as an appropriate age. Darkenwald and Merriam (1982) have also stated eighteen as the age for adult learning

However, there are those like Johnston and Revera who have stated twenty-one and over as an appropriate age. According to research in the neurosciences this would be the most likely age that brain development begins to be recognized. It is true that development continues for many years but at twenty-one there are signs of development that are so obvious that they mark a new stage for the individual.

While there may be doubts regarding the timing of social changes, be it independence, gaining employment, accepting social roles, marriage or becoming a parent, there is hardly doubt about the timing of brain development if health is not a factor. Research has now made it possible to pin down some specifics of brain development and age. These specifics mark a clear distinction between the child and the adult. Blomm, Beal, and Kupfer (2003) agree on age twenty because it takes that long for the brain to self—construct and it is this period onto the fifties that must be considered the prime of life.

There is enough evidence gathered on brain development to prove age twenty and over as being the time of brain change from the underdeveloped to the developed. Bloom et. al., has placed this development in three stages: the first is the stage of wiring, this is the childhood years, the second is the stage of adolescence when the frontal lobe is developing, and third is the final stage when the brain is concerned with plasticity. It is at this stage that the brain is ready to learn about life, form new habits, adjust to new situations, and learn new ways. It is at this stage that the brain is ready for adult education.

The adult brain relies on this plasticity for long-term memory. At twenty and older, the brain begins to send signal transmissions throughout the entire nervous system. At twenty and older the frontal lobes become fully myelinated helping the young adult to overcome emotional outbursts, and control impulsive behavior. This also helps the learning process. Older adults make fewer changes in their degree plan at college because they have reasoned out their program carefully. Young people make their choices according to how they feel at the time, changing their degree plan many times. This is because long term decision making is difficult to do if the pre-frontal cortex is underdeveloped.

There are other distinctions relating to the adult brain that have profound implications for andragogy. Carter (1999) says that as we get older our brain functions become more rigid, thus we become more distinctive individuals. She also notes that as adults our mental landscapes are so different that no two of us will understand anything in quite the same way. What is important to one adult is not so to another. Teachers of adults confront this frequently, and many adults will show there frustration over a subject they have no interest in. Children, on the other hand, are more apt to have like interest in the same subject. It makes teaching them in the same class-room as a group a lot simpler.

The adult begins to experience a graduation of the brain as early as age twenty (See Table I). Biological changes begin to take place that do not occur in the child. Adults begin to lose neurons, but not as much as once believed. Because of this loss of neurons the brain size begins to decline, this happens at a different rate for each person, it is slower in some people than in others. These changes begin to affect cognitive decline over a period of time. These declines may be in the area of spatial ability, speed of perception, decision making, response, and even memory.

For adults the cortex that controls visualizing, listening, and thinking about words, thinking and speaking words, which is affect by age and as a result slows down but does not halt the learning process. This becomes very obvious in a class that is combined with youth, young adults and older adults. It will take a little longer for the older adult to process the information because of brain changes. This is not to say the adults are not learning, but that they need more time to learn.

When it comes to the working memory the adult uses a different region of the brain. The child uses the prefrontal cortices, according to Restak (2001), without thinking of economizing the usage of the brain. The adult's brain has less usage when trying to remember something. The adult is more efficient in the use of the brain, using a smaller area. For the same task the child and the adult are using their brains in a different way. Adults are only interested in remembering the things that are absolutely relevant to daily life and survival.

Another distinct difference with adults is the change in blood flow in the brain. Less blood flow to the visual cortex explains the need for reading glasses and the preference for books with larger print. Less blood flow to the cingulated region explains the slow response at times to external stimuli. Loud noises, dim lights, extreme temperatures become a distraction to the adult student.

Again, all these stages of graduation in the brain, make adults who they are, unique individuals. So children will be more alike socially, physically, mentally, and even be able to relate to certain learning tasks with very little life experience. An adult class on the other hand will have students very different from each other socially, physically, and mentally. The older we get the more diversified we become.

A final area of graduation is that of memory. We are reminded by the research that no one will be able to remember a story or commit a name to memory in the same way they did at age sixteen, by the time they reach age seventy-six, due to the fact that our mental functions change as we age. Long-term memory gained through life, however, will always be there. It will not be lost. The recall time will increase as we age, we will need more time to jog that memory. It is the belief of Bloom, et al. that this slowing of recall begins as early as age twenty. The signal transmission throughout the brain slows with age. This makes timed tests very difficult for many adults. It may not be that they do not know the answers but it is the limited time in which they are asked to answer the questions that poses a problem.

This information is not being related to discourage adult learning but rather to demonstrate the important differences between the adult and the child in a neurological context. Adults can be trained to improvise or compensate for losses, learning is still possible even with age related changes.

FORMER PERSPECTIVES ON ADULT INTELLIGENCE

The learning of adults and their level of intelligence has always been held in question. Can adults learn beyond a certain age? At what age do adults begin to lose brain plasticity? Does intelligence decline with age? These are only some of the questions asked when exploring learning in conjunction with aging. In the past, the emphasis has been on debilitating aspects of aging as it relates to learning. Also, age old myths with just enough truth to "make the barb stick" (Kidd, 1967, p. 20) find their way into the former perspectives, if not in whole, in part; if not in theory, in practice.

Educators have expressed their frustration in trying to understand adult learning and intelligence. Kidd (1967) stated that there is no answer to the question as to how adults learn and Lovell (1980) claimed that psychology is unable "to provide a comprehensive and closely integrated theoretical account of how human adult learning comes about" (p. 30).

Lemme (1999) believes much of the lack of understanding regarding adult learning and cognitive development is beginning to pass. As research in adult cognitive functions flourishes, Lemme states there is a need for theory that can integrate the various findings and make a clear sense of the meaning of it all.

In an attempt to move in this direction, neuroandragogy first promotes strongly the positive notion of adult learning capabilities and the fact that maturing in age is an asset to learning possibilities. Neuroandragogy looks beyond the myths and the decrementalist model of inevitable decline in intellect. Neuroandragogy also searches out empirical studies that support the facts that aging must be seen as growth and not decline, as improvement and not regression, and quite capable of compensating for any loss.

When learning and aging come up for investigation by researchers, the mapping of intellectual functioning usually comes into question. However, when adult intelligence is questioned there is always the concern as to what is being measured. This concern arises because the concept of intelligence was first directed to childhood achievement in the classroom. Birren (in Darkenwald & Merriam, 1982) points out that as life changes the concept of intelligence changes too. Intelligence for children is the variable which governs how well one masters the work of the classroom, it is the mastering of the school curriculum. While for the adult, intelligence may be how effective they function in relating to other people, especially with words; how well they are able to solve the problems of life and their ability to learn new concepts.

E. L. Thorndike's investigation into adult learning led him to make conclusions that were contrary to the popular theories of his time. He believed adults did not become less intelligent as they aged. Other researchers followed in the steps of Thorndike, investigating adult intelligence. Horn and Catell developed the concept of fluid and crystallized intelligence, Baltes has examined reserved plasticity and Gardener multiple intelligence. However, most of Thorndike's tests were based on timed performances of motor tasks which may not have been very meaningful to the adults. Examples of these tests are; right hand users learning to write with the left hand, or, the memorizing of an artificial language that was entirely useless to the adult. As a result his work has been greatly criticized as having questionable factors. Other methods have been used since but questions of concern regarding what is being measured, or how it's being measured, are still being asked.

NEW PERSPECTIVES ON ADULT INTELLIGENCE

New insights carry impressive implication for adult education and educators for the formulating of new education practice and policy making. Carmichael (2000) observed that we must begin to revise virtually all the old notions or theories relating to human learning and memory. Neuroandragogy seeks to do just this by redefining intelligence. Originally adult intelligence was defined by measuring memory loss or cognitive decline in older adults. Now neuroandragogy seeks to pursue avenues that will express the adult's lifetime experiences, expertise and their problem solving skills. Adult intelligence must no longer be defined by what is measured on an intelligence scale (which usually has a set of responses that demonstrate intelligent behavior as determined by the test designer). All adults are different in behavior according to culture, age or just through the need to survive, thus there can be no universal test of intelligence.

Adult intelligence must be defined according to brain plasticity and not brain stability. Santrock (1985) declares that rather than evaluating plasticity, standardized tests of intelligence are designed to measure the stable condition of the tested, with the majority designed for younger individuals. It is now being agreed on that plasticity in the adult is an important part of intellectual graduation. As seen in previous chapters, Baltes and his colleagues have been in search of ways to measure this plasticity, which they regard as latent reserves. Baltes' concern is the testing of the strengths of adult intellectual graduation and brain plasticity mainly because this has sparked disagreement among psychometric theorists. Santrock says this disagreement becomes obvious when it relates to the degree of plasticity in intellectual functioning during late life. Several tests now being used on adult subjects are having success in proving that reserved plasticity in aging adults does exist.

Neuroandragogy supports the view that plasticity is important for adults to function into later life and that many cognitive activities are unused or under exercised in most individual adults. It is the using of these abilities over time that improve performance in intellectual activities.

It is unfair to measure the intelligence of adults by administering timed tests. IQ tests are timed and seek specific answers for specific questions. This presents a problem for many adults who for one, are intimidated by tests, especially when timed. Many adults have also been out of the classroom for many years and have developed certain learning habits of their own that may not fit the standard testing system. One such habit observed by Darkenwald and Merriam is the practice of omission when in doubt. Adults have learned how to pace themselves in verbal activity. This results in caution when asked to respond to a question or give advice on a situation. Having to do this in a given time may get nil response from the adult. Adults make more errors of omission than commission because adults would rather not respond at all than respond with a wrong answer. Darkenwald and Merriam make mention of Eisdorfer's discovery that older subjects under test stress may experience a high arousal state, measurable by free fatty acids in the blood. This inhibits a speedy response to test questions.

Slow response to timed test is also a result of adults processing information at a much slower rate, the older they become the slower it gets. Several reasons were mentioned earlier that may bring on slow processing. Restak (2001) believes that as we get older more time must be given for the processing of information as the working memory begins to lose some of its capacity, and gets to a point where it may only be able to process one point at a time. Much of the speed of processing information however may be dependent upon the adult's lifestyle. Disuse of information can make for slow recall. Interferences in a normal lifestyle is also a factor. This may include social, physical or mental situations. Neurological and neurochemical abnormalities can also hinder the speed of information processing.

Neuroandragogy is in favor of developing a framework that promotes the intelligence of adults outside of timed test. It was Elias, Elias and Elias (1977) who said, "intelligence is clearly not 'that which is measured by intelligence tests'" (p. 71). While Restak (2001) in agreement said that slow processing of information is a poor way to judge intelligence since many adults may be slow at processing due to the overloading of information to the brain. Restak believes that if adults and youth are timed on the same test, in most cases the youth will win. But if the time factor is removed and each contestant has an equal grasp of the facts, more than likely the older person will perform just as well as the youth.

Kline (1998) calls for new ways to measure intelligence because the old system has fallen short in many ways. Kline writes that psychometrics has isolated several ability and personality factors which hold sound evidence for their validity and psychological meaning and significance. Kline not only abhors the fact that these personality factors have never been a part of the instrument, but that the instrument itself is flawed because it is far different from measurement used in the natural sciences. The lack in clear units of measurement and real zeros is seen as a problem by Kline. As it is right now, the assumption of psychometrics has been that measurement is the assigning of numbers to variables. Kline observes that in addition to this problem is the fact that the philosophical assumptions are antithetical to other sciences.

Kline (1998) continues to point out that psychometrics' assumptions are based on operationalism, meaning that a variable is defined by its method of measurement, this is not the norm in science. Kline shows that science endeavors to stick to the notion of there being an objective truth which science sets out to find. This, Kline believes, is absent in psychometrics where relativism is evident. Kline insists that psychometrics should measure accurately and with precision as has been done in the natural sciences. He calls for clear theories and indisputable findings to develop from psychometrics, which are "similar to those found in the chemistry and physics of engineering or the biology and biochemistry of medicine" (p. 179). Kline does not regard psychometrics as a complete failure, but as a science that needs to develop accurate meaningful measurements. He concludes that psychometrics must become more experimental and biological in nature to arrive at scientific measures of its variables.

Neuoandragogy also creates a paradigm shift from the assumptions of adult experiences and assumptions of development, to the scientific facts of the importance of experience and the effect on the adult brain. Neuroandragogy is in agreement that the adult's life experience is one of many distinctions between the adult and the child in the learning process. However, this new paradigm explains the experiences of the adult, not in importance according to quantity or quality, but rather by the importance it plays in the development of the adult's perceptual and cognitive abilities, according to Elbert, Heim and Rockstroh of the University of Kanstanz, Germany. These scientists observe that experience increases the skill of an individual through cortical reorganization, making every new experience help in the making of individual differences. These and other scientists now state that experiences help the adult to transfer information from short-term memory to long-term memory, guiding and solving particular learning problems. These problem solving skills get better as we get older. When youth is compared with adulthood they come up short on experience.

Neuroandragogy, as a new direction for studying adult education and learning, is therefore correct in the use of proven science that has biological facts, measurable experiments and clear theories

The following are a few examples of the latest findings that are being integrated into the theories of adult learning and adult intelligence:

1. The "window of opportunity" regarding learning is now being challenged and it is being agreed on to be longer than first believed, in some cases life long, depending on the learning adventure (Andreasen, 2000).

2. Brain plasticity is now expected to be a lifelong possibility, which is in contrast to earlier studies that indicated a decline in intellectual capacity as aging occurred. New findings now indicate that intelligence does decline but not at the speed once believed. It is now concluded that intellectual decline occurs relatively late in life for the healthy adult (Shaie, as cited in Tennant & Pog son, 1995).

3. Old views held that the brain is like a computer functioning like a linear or parallel-processing machine. New views reject this comparison but prefer to describe the brain as a self-organizing system that changes with use through out its lifetime. The brain's neuron connections are loose, flexible, webbed and redundant (On Purpose Associates, 2001).

4. Old views held that there is no brain cell growth after birth, that we are born with all the brain cells we will ever have, and with chronological aging brain cells are lost. New studies now challenge the conventional views. Scientists such as Erikson, McEwen, Gould, Gage, Ebner and others have demonstrated new brain cell growth in adult animals and adult human beings alike. This new growth is known as neurogenesis.

5. The left brain, right brain concept has been replaced by the left hemisphere, right hemisphere concept with the view that both hemispheres are needed for correct intellectual functions.

NEW PERSPECTIVES ON PSYCHOMETRICS

The concern of research conducted by developmental psychologists up until the 1980's includes recovering intelligence to its former level of performance and a certain degree of plasticity in late adulthood (Tennant & Pogson, 1995; Salthouse, 1985; Berger & Thompson, 1994; Baltes, Kliegl, Dittman-Kohli, 1988).

Recent research in developmental psychology and gerontology has shown new concerns such as "the search for latent reserves and plasticity of aging" (Baltes, 1999, p. 24), and the "biology of intelligence" or measurement of intelligence in terms that are physiological rather than psychological", (Kline, 1998, p. 182). Research in cognitive neuroscience seeks to answer these concerns in studies covering brain development, learning, memory, the capacity for plasticity, and the neurological development of intelligence (D'Arcangelo, 2000; Fischer & Rose, 1998; Sylvester, 1998; Sprenger, 1999).

New research in developmental psychology seeks to relocate the boundaries of plasticity. Between the 1920's and 1980's, the research focused upon demonstrating plasticity as a strategy by which the limits and boundaries of development were identified. This focus began to change in the late 1980's from demonstrating the normal range of intellectual functioning to revealing the limits of performance. Using the research strategy known as 'testing-the-limits' explained by Lawton and Salthouse as, "The systematic application of (a) variations in modes of assessment, (b) methods of intervention aimed at identifying latent reserve capacity, and (c) strategies of identification of the mechanisms involved in growth and decline" (1998, p. 103).

This research effort seeks to determine age-correlated changes in the limits of adult intellectual ability. In the process, three aspects of plasticity are distinguished by Lawton and Salthouse: baseline performance, baseline reserve capacity, and developmental reserve capacity:

1. Baseline performance indicates a person's initial level of performance on a given task without intervention or special treatment.

2. Baseline reserve capacity denotes the upper range of the person's potential, that which may be called "maximum" performance.

3. The developmental reserve capacity in performance is accomplished when help is given to the baseline reserve capacity through intervention (1998).

Baltes (1999) states that "The third common theoretical orientation, the identification of the range and limits of plasticity and reserve capacity in old age, is more recent" (p 24). He explains that it was developed in reaction to the long standing position, which is prominent especially among biologists, that loss, in the ability to adapt, is the essential feature of aging. Baltes observes that with this new development more attention is now being directed to the "identification of potential gains and latent reserves of old age". Plasticity is now classified with "two faces," the psychological and sociological. In this new "dual" research, Baltes believes it is expressed in the juxtaposition of "range and limits" of plasticity (p. 24).

Baltes (1999) explains that according to former information, aging is typically associated "with increasing limits to, and restrictions in, physical, neurobiological, mental, and social capacities" (p. 24). However, within the past decade gerontological research has presented impressive evidence of plasticity and pointed to sizable untapped reserves of older adults in many different domains including biochemical, physical, cognitive, and social functioning (Reinhold, et al., 1989).

"The search for latent reserves and plasticity of aging", says Baltes (1999, p. 24), is paramount in importance. Without an understanding of the current occurrences of aging, our society may continue to underestimate the potential of the last segments of the aging person's life span (1999).

A final point to be made for research into the twenty-first century is empirical findings that mental abilities can be improved by training, experience, or exercise; this has been of keen interest to researchers. Baltes, in his 1987 report on the notion of the plasticity of adult intellectual development, began to attest to these conclusions. Some researchers are of the opinion that adults possess the reserve capacity to raise their levels of performance of fluid intelligence (Rybash, Roodink and Santrock, 1991).

Baltes (as cited in Salthouse, 1998) reports his findings of cognitive training:

The cognitive training research conducted with older adults offered strong evidence of sizeable plasticity. After a fairly brief program of cognitive practice, many older adults (age range, sixty-eighty years) exhibited levels of performance comparable with those observed in many "untreated" younger adults (p. 102).

A similar finding has been found in research dealing with aging and dementia. It indicates that mental training or "gymnastics" are important in keeping neural networks alive and responsible for forming new ones. This research suggests mastering new challenges to keep the brain functioning. The simple everyday task of reading, writing, working on the computer or studying in one's field does not help as much as tackling something for which one is completely unfamiliar (Scherer, 1997).

Fisher and Rose (1998) agree with the research and add that this training of the intellect must continue throughout life. They propose the individual's level of skill and understanding depends pervasively on the contextual support for high-level functioning. This, they believe, must come through effective teaching, and even into later ages. The effective textual presentation must powerfully support high-level functioning. If this support is removed, it will lead to a natural rapid drop in the level of understanding.

In the past, conclusions of adult intelligence have been drawn from life-span developmental psychology, behaviorist and cognitive theorist (Woodruff-Pak, 1988; Darkenwald & Merriam, 1982). Kline (1998) believes it's time to move to a new level in psychometrics, so that an understanding of the physiological along with the psychological may be gained (1998).

Biological studies in brain plasticity provide physiological information needed for the forward move suggested by Kline. The value and concepts of brain plasticity for the learning and education of adults were examined earlier.

Table 1
The Graduation Scale of the Adult Brain

Brain Characteristics	Age of Change	Graduation Process
The size of the matured brain	Early twenties	A gyrification (GI) of 2.6
The emotional measurement of the matured brain	Early twenties	Begins to be able to plan in advance in a logical and systematic way, with less emotion and impulse.
Graduation of neurons	Early twenties	Increase in neurons by as much as 100 trillion in number. Loss of cells also occur at rates that differ for each adult.
Thickness of cortex	Twenties to eighties	From a thickness of 4.0mm to 3.12mm by age eighty two.
Graduation of blood flow to the brain	Late forties to early fifties	Changes of blood to the brain begins, the older one gets, the more diffused the changes are.
Graduation of memory	Twenties to late life	The retrieval process of stored information begins to slow down. Memory loss develops at a rate of a few milliseconds per year.
Graduation of cognition	Sixty and older	Some cognitive graduation occurs but not as severe as once expected. One third of adults at this age do not experience significant graduation.
Graduation of cognition	Sixty and older	Some cognitive graduation occurs but not as severe as once expected. One third of adults at this age do not experience significant graduation.

Table 1
The Graduation Scale of the Adult Brain (Continued)

Graduation of fluid intelligence	Seventy and older	Some brain functions are challenged at this age, and may get weaker. Examples are memory, object manipulation, inductive reasoning, attention and processing capabilities.
Graduation of brain use	Twenties through life	The child and youth uses a fairly large area for memory task. The adult relies on a smaller area of the brain, conserving on brain usage.
Graduation of the learning process	Twenties through life	The learning process begins to slow down, but continues through life.

12

FROM THEORY TO PRACTICE

Most adults enroll in higher or continued education mainly for economic reasons. Education for many has served as a means to an end. Teachers of adults have also seen education in this light and therefore teach to meet these needs. It is therefore difficult to convince the general public that education in itself works as an instrument for improvement that is highly beneficial even without specific economic gain.

Neuroandragogy seeks to promote adult education not only for its socioeconomic benefits but also for its overall relevance to better brain health, brain cell growth, enhanced brain reserve, and increased brain plasticity. The practice of brain-based education at the adult level is needed to achieve this goal.

Several years ago, educator and educational psychologist, John Bruer (1999) stated that brain-based education was an idea whose time had not yet arrived. His reasons then were that we did not know enough about the way the brain works to tie it into educational practice and policy making. Bruer said, "we know only a little about learning, thinking, and remembering at the level of neural circuits, or synapses; we know very little about how the brain thinks, remembers, and learns" (1999, p. 650). Bruer held that more must be known in order to base educational changes on brain studies and that educators should stick to what they know, psychology.

This book disagrees with Bruer's conclusions and tries instead to highlight any biological science and documented results in brain research that tends to aid in the better practice of adult education and learning. As a result this chapter bridges research, theory, and practice.

TEACHING TOWARDS BRAIN HEALTH

It is clear that all adults experience some type of mental decline as they age. Some from natural aging and others from illness and disease. However, adult educators must not use this natural occurrence to form decrementalist views of inevitable decline which is often found in the study of psychology and human development. Mental decline is a common concern among adults, but teachers must give hope to adult students by promoting the view of continued potential and possible compensation for natural loss.

It should also be clear that the decline in healthy adults is no where as swift as once believed, but that it happens over a long period. We now know that much of our concerns regarding mental decline, such as memory loss and recall inability, to some extent, result from old studies that equated aging with mental decline that came because of neuron failure. Now we know according to neurobiologist Caleb Finch, *The Aging Brain* (2001), that if there is no disease that causes loss of nerve cells, then most if not all our neurons remain healthy until we die. It is now believed that cognitive decline such as age-related memory loss is not due to neuron loss but instead to complex chemical interactions in the brain occurring as we age.

For example, it has been suggested the plaque and tangles on the brain are the cause of Alzheimer's disease. However, a recent study published in the Journal of Neurophysiology notes a research result of the examination of the brains of elderly people. It was discovered that these elderly people functioned fully while alive yet they were found with large numbers of plaques and tangles looking exactly like those attributed to Alzheimer's disease. None of the elderly who were examined displayed any symptoms of Alzheimer's disease. New research is now suggesting that this disease may be caused by inflammatory processes which result from aging.

Finch (The Aging Brain, 2001) found amyloid aggregates on the brain—a hard deposit on the brain caused from degenerated tissues—resulting from inflammatory proteins in the brain. Finch states that inflammatory proteins occur to some extent in all maturing adults. However, soluble amyloid aggregates are formed in the parts of the brain usually affected by Alzheimer's disease. This was also found in the hippocampus which is responsible for forming new memory. This, Finch believes, gets in the way of long-term memory some length of time before brain cells are killed by it. Research also suggests that as we age we lose dopamine, a brain chemical associated with pleasure and reward found in the regions of the brain believed to relate to cognition. However, not every adult experiences these changes at the same pace.

What is most intriguing to the study of neuroandragogy is the news that the rate of these changes may be hastened or slowed by the adult depending on their choice of life style. Adult educators must encourage good health habits that will discourage this decline.

Several lifestyle factors have been named by researchers that either speeds up the aging process or slows it down. These include hypertension which speeds up normal brain shrinkage and head trauma mimicking Alzheimer's disease. On the other hand exercise improves cognitive abilities, rest protects against age-related chronic illness including memory loss, and very important is the correct diet. The factor of education and its effect on the aging brain is of great interest to the study of neuroandragogy. Studies comparing college graduates and adults who did not attend college are concluding that those who use their brain do not lose it as quickly.

Although some scientists hesitate to classify the brain as a muscle, the patterns of connectivity are formed by repetition, a pattern used to build muscle. Using a repetitive pattern in our daily life makes synaptic connections stronger and broader. The connections between neurons in the system that is well used become stronger. Guttman (2003) says a recent study has shown that cognitive challenge faced by adult rodent brains actually created new neurons. The human adult brain stands the chance to also experience the growth of new neurons if faced with regular challenges.

ADULT EDUCATORS MUST TEACH WITH AN UNDERSTANDING OF HOW NEW BRAIN CELLS ARE FORMED AND NEW MEMORY CREATED

Adult educators now have access to information that will give them a better understanding of the neural development of adult learners and the myths that once existed regarding adults and learning. Teachers of adults have an opportunity to change the landscape of their student's brain in more ways than one; they can help the increase of brain cells, and brain reserve.

Increasing brain cells.

Brain cell growth has been confirmed in the brains of human adults, even at fifty to seventy years of age. This growth has been located in the hippocampus. As you may remember from readings in an earlier chapter, the hippocampus is responsible for long-term memory which is pertinent to learning new information. Erikson and Gage, who discovered this brain cell growth, are of the opinion that education has a major role to play in the prevention of Alzheimer's disease (Carper, 2000). Adreasen's (2001) reports agree strongly with that of Erikson and Gage. She says there is a positive correlation between high education and the absence of brain dementia, including Alzheimer's disease. Carmichael (2002) also reports similar findings which states that the more connections made between brain cells through education and interesting work the more resistant they are to Alzheimer's disease. The more cells are formed the less likely it is to suffer from brain dementia. Researchers now conclude that the risk of cognitive decline increases with less education and lowers with more. Figure 22 demonstrates the effect dementia can have on neurons.

Adult education must use all elements necessary to encourage cell growth. In part, this growth is the result of an enriched education environment which encompasses teaching with novelty, teaching with controversy and in conflict to the standard beliefs held by adult students, and employing meaningful activities or practices that involve all five senses.

Adult teachers must also involve their students in the activity of designing curriculum. For the purpose of brain cell growth curriculums must be created to encourage complexity, novelty, and creativity. This must all be done with the students' interest in mind, their experience and expertise. Variety must not be forgotten because no two adults are alike.

Encouraging memory.

When new brain cells have been created there must be a plan to keep them alive. New brain cells are kept alive by the law that states we use it or we lose it. It is true that adults are most interested in learning things they can use right away, things they can apply to life right now, not ten years later. The teacher of adults must be able to encourage immediate usage of information gained so that newly formed cells survive. Long-term memory relies on the survival of these new cells.

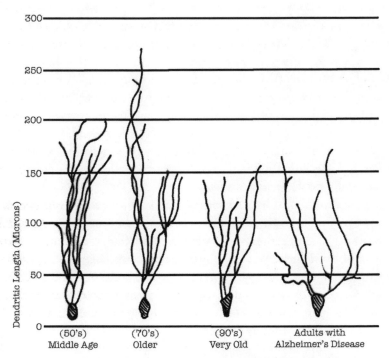

Figure 22 A demonstration of normal hippocampus neurons and
neurons affected by Alzheimer's disease

Shorts, of Rutgers University and Gould, of Princeton demonstrated the importance of the "use it or lose it" law in a recent study. Both researchers found that their study on rats'brains and the gaining of new brain cells required hippocampus-related learning to improve the survival rate of new brain cells. Observations made by these researchers are important to the understanding of new brain cell survival. New brain cells are now believed to die within a matter of weeks of their generation (Hyland, 2003). Once new cells are gained they are kept alive by learning activities that affect the hippocampus. According to Margery Silver and Thomas Perls (WedMD, 2003) for this to happen the mind must be kept active by new activities that create exercises for different parts of the brain.

Examples include, learning a new language, learning to play an instrument, writing an autobiography, and volunteering. Such activities, they claim, develop new connections between the various parts of the brain, which also strengthen and prevent any deficit from emerging during daily functions.

It is important that adults learn through new challenges. Teachers of adults must impress upon the adult learner the significance of departing from the beaten track of familiar subjects to exploring new horizons.

Silver (WebMD, 2003) greatly encouraged by her research of two hundred men and women whose ages were one hundred or older, says the myths and common thinking of dementia by age one hundred is just that—only a myth. She concludes that the brain must continue to be exercised into old age. She holds that this will help retain the ability to think, predicting whether one retains independence or not. She observes that while people can often compensate for physical disabilities with various devices and assistance, to do so for mental abilities would be much more difficult.

ADULT EDUCATORS MUST TEACH TO INCREASE BRAIN RESERVE

Brain reserve is gained by the constant challenging of the brain through life. Gatz (2003) is of the opinion that having more education creates a good chance of having more intellectual ability and greater brain reserve; however, the process of developing this reserve must be lifelong.

Adult education should include training that will increase the brain reserve of the adult. This is done by first determining the limitations of the intellectual abilities of the adult and then developing a program to increase those abilities. To know the limitations of the adult intellectual ability we must test for three things:

1. Baseline performance, which is the initial level of ones performance on any given task, be it academic or practical without any intervention or any special treatment.

2. Baseline reserve capacity test will show the upper range or upper level of ones potential. This is seen as the maximum performance. Here adults get a second chance to prove themselves, they get to retake the same test, with the leniency of more time and with a knowledge of what is on the test.

3. Developmental reserve takes the test one step further. Here the baseline reserve is given help through intervention such as, pre-test training, exercise or practice at the particular skill to be tested.

The third step is our immediate concern. This effort helps improve on the brain reserve that already exists, increasing plasticity or the adaptability of the brain. Baltes (as cited in Salthouse, 1998) reports that cognitive training conducted with older adults, ages ranging from sixty to eighty, offered strong evidence of sizeable plasticity. Many of these adults were able to perform as well as younger adults who received no treatment. Now we know that new limits can be established in the physical, mental, neurobiological and social capacities of adult life. Adult education must utilize methods that tap into the untapped reserves of the adult in the many different domains including; biochemical, physical, cognitive, and social functioning.

Adult Educators Must Include High Frequency Activities In The Lesson Plan

We now know that best results in memory storage and recall are derived from meaningful education, brain activity, and personal experiences. A very common complaint among adult learners is that conventional education is not very meaningful. In any given academic program every adult is able to mention several classes that had no meaning to them. It is difficult to learn and remember if the subject has no meaning and is presented without incorporating brain activity.

Hebb (1943) explained in his learning theory that memory is produced when there is activity to strengthen the relationship between the synapses. Memory and learning are dependent on synaptic plasticity, the following points are examples of the learning brain and why it needs high frequency activity for optimal learning to take place.

High Frequency Activity Strengthens Synapses (LTP) While Low Frequency Activity Weakens Synapses (LTD).

As discussed earlier, this includes complex biochemical processes which involve the actions of neurotransmitters and postsynaptic receptors. As demonstrated before LTP (long term potentiation) plays a great role in the mechanism of learning. It is the strong stimulation of a presynaptic neuron that in turn strengthens the synapse. If there are weakly stimulated synapses activated at the same time, the strong stimulation will strengthen them. It is this strong stimulation that leads to strong depolarization of the postsynaptic neuron. This depolarization triggers the LTP (Solomon, Berg, and Martin, 1999).

LTP is a result of high frequency activities that strengthen synapses. These synapses are responsible for creating new cells. Memory, in turn, is made by these individual cells; a memory is formed when a pattern of action is repeated frequently, or if there is a circumstance that encourages the memory to be encoded. This is a result of the high activity or the firing of a group of neurons which soon develop the tendency to do so again and again, as demonstrated earlier. This increases over time (Carter, 1998). Hebb says, the neurons that fire together stay together. Carter says these neurons fire in synchrony, by setting one off, the others go off too.

This high frequency activity causes neurons to fire faster giving off a greater electrical charge which, in all likelihood, will trigger a neighbor neuron. When the neighbor has been stimulated to fire, a chemical change is now on its surface which makes it very sensitive to stimulation from the same neighbor, thus LTP has occurred (Carter, 1998).

When new brain cells have been created they stay in a state of readiness for hours or days, but, as stated before, if there is no stimulation for these new cells they soon die. Carter (1998) stresses that if the firing of the first cell happens again within a specific time, either hours or days, the neighboring cells will respond even if the firing is slow. Every firing that occurs in this period of time is of great importance, for each makes the cell more receptive. If this is repeated in synchronous firing, neurons will bind together so that the littlest activity in one triggers all those that have become a part of the family associated with the firing. A memory is then formed (1998).

Long-term memory relies on more than a brief activity or situation. The more influence upon the memory, the better the memory.

Examples of High Frequency Activity.

Episodic memory is a result of high frequency activity; it strengthens the synapses causing long-term memory to develop. Carter (1998) illustrates this concept with a brief story of someone awaiting the return of a son or daughter from a boating trip. As this person waits at the shore sipping a cool drink, listening to music and overlooking the sea, several things begin to make a mega-pattern woven from the elementary motifs created by a pattern described to be fear, such as:

1. The taste of the cold drink;

2. The experience of the blue sea;

3. The sound of music;

4. A pattern of the face of the children and the last time they were seen;

5. A pattern of a last late home experience;

6. Thoughts of lifeguards and life jackets; and

7. What may be said when they finally arrive.

Carter (1998) says this constellation of neural activity comes and goes, changing from time to time, but the general theme remains. Some mega-patterns remain in the long-term memory while others eventually fade away. The experiences that stand out most, like "sharp points of light" (p. 162) are stored as long-term memories in the hippocampus where they are believed to be held for as long as two to three years. In this period of time the hippocampus relays the stored experiences to the cortex. With each rehearsal of the experiences, it is etched deeper and deeper into the cortex. If this activity continues over a period of time, soon the hippocampus is no longer needed for the recall of the experience because the memory is firmly established in the cortex. Without this exercise the experience is eventually forgotten.

Carter (1998) explains that much of the hippocampal relay is believed to occur while we sleep, for dreams consist partly of reminders of events that occurred during the day. It's the hippocampus firing up information to the cortex about the day's activity.

Like other researchers, Carter (1998) wonders why some brain patterns remain potent while others disappear. One answer given by research is that while high frequency activity strengthens synapses, low frequency activity weakens synapses (Myers, 2002). Carter explains it as the result of emotional excitement or its absence. Excitement, says Carter, is brought about by a surge of excitatory neurotransmitters that increase the firing response of neurons in designated parts of the brain. To prevent a nasty recurrence the brain will remember a former experience, such as being burnt by a hot stove, that must not be repeated, or something very nice like the taste of ice cream, that will be sought after in the future.

Episodes destined for long-term memory do not go straight to the hippocampus but first to the cortex and over a period of two years these memories are still very fragile and can be wiped out before they become permanent memory. Normally during this time the hippocampus will keep replaying these episodes to the cortex. If this fails to happen the memory is then lost. Bringing a long-term fact to mind causes the activation of the frontal and temporal cortical areas; episodic recollections are found in these regions as well as in several others. The hippocampus does not give up all its long-term memory to the cortical storage area. An example of this is fear, which is encoded in the hippocampal neurons. Even though the hippocampus has been detected for storing personal memories, episodes of fear are found to be stored in the amygdala ("the limbic nucleus that registers fear," Carter, 1998, p. 166).

LOW FREQUENCY ACTIVITIES MUST BE AVOIDED

Carter (1998) gives an example of the taste of tannin found in wine. At first taste, it may be registered as part of a general red 'winey' taste. Here the association between the neurons that momentarily unite to create the taste experience will become weak and may even disappear if the tannin is not tasted again for awhile. If the taste is practiced, the tannin neurons will retain some attraction for each other; the taste will then be recognized. If it became a habit to detect tannin from other flavors in the wine, the neural pattern created by the tannin will be acti vated repeatedly and strengthened. The taste of tannin becomes familiar and instantly detectable.

However, says Carter, this memory of tannin is considered elementary. If, when acquiring the taste, a name is added so as to help in the memory of the taste, this label becomes another chance to strengthen the memory neurons. The memory of tannin will then include the taste and the label. So when it is said that the wine is high in tannin you will know how it will taste. Another element that could be improve the memory is, adding to the existing knowledge, the role tannin plays in wine making or its chemical structure. Carter claims the more aspects to the memory makeup, the more useful it becomes and the easier it is to retrieve because more handles are created by which to pull out the full memory, storage. Such memory, says Carter, usually ends up in what is called the semantic memory. This memory is information we gain independent of our relationship to it. At first, however, these memories of things are laid down as part of a bigger construct that includes the personal. For example, one will remember where he/ she was when the tannin was tasted, who one was with and what was said about it. But if there is no significance to these incidents found later on, the memory will eventually fail. What is left is the knowledge of tannin itself. This, says Carter, is the happening of all things we know. The important things remain, usually these are the bare but useful facts, while the marginal aspects fall by the way.

Marginal notes may fall into the category of low frequency activity, known as LTD (long-term depression), which bear less and less importance to the individual. The LTD weakens the synapses and memory begins to slip away. These marginal notes are usually reflective of the semantic or short-term declarative memory which usually seeks only to store the general knowledge of facts, words and the meanings of these words.

When the name of the authors of popular books are remembered or other details of life, it means that there has been careful storage of a large amount of information, well organized for rapid retrieval. Many adults complain of TOT (tip-of-the-tongue) experience where memory is close but not quite there, another case of LTD. This, says Balota, et al., (2000), is the most common memory complaint of older adults, wherein one tries to explicitly recall the name of a person or a low-frequency word to fit the appropriate context. TOT leaves one with the feeling of knowing but not being able to recall. This problem in older adults has been recorded in diary studies of memory, and in experimental studies.

Neuroandragogy is a move in the direction of understanding the working of the memory functions of the adult. Teaching and training with that knowledge becomes important. The old methods used in the past that did not encourage long-term memory must be changed for new effective methods. Lectures must be accompanied with activities of prior discovery. Personal reading must be accompanied with interviews and dialogue, with others who have similar interest, prior to lectures. Research with relevant life connections must be encouraged and new approaches to life's problems must be introduced with relevant connections to the lecture.

13

SUMMARY

THE TENETS OF NEUROANDRAGOGY

The framework of neuroandragogy focuses purposefully on the adult brain, its cognitive functions and its graduation, all in relationship to the education of the adult and the adult's learning habits. In this final chapter, the tenets of neuroandragogy are enumerated.

1. Neuroandragogy and Its Relationship to Pedagogy

It has been made very clear through research in neuroscience and cognitive neuroscience that the brain of the child differs from the developed brain of the adult. This difference is seen in the way children process learning versus the way adults process learning. Neuroandragogy offers strong rationale for the science of adult education and learning to be a separate field of study and not to be treated as a continuum of childhood education and learning. Childhood education must no longer be favored by researchers and scholars of education at the expense of adult education. There must now be a fair chance given to both pedagogy and andragogy. It must no longer be said that adult education is under studied, under researched and under funded.

2. Neuroandragogy and Research

Access to research data, tools and organizations provides a base from which to create neuroandragogical constructs. This creation, in turn, provides results that are beneficial to other sciences. Linking sciences together which have already accomplished proven empirical research is not new and proves beneficial to new learning. Research in the neurosciences has now provided great opportunities to tie education with science that can reform the field of education.

3. The Chronological Age of the Adult

Differentiating the adult from the child by the use of chronological age has posed a huge problem for education (Darkenwald & Merriam, 1982). Some adult educators have placed the age of adult students at eighteen (Savicevic, 1988), while others have recommended twenty-one,(Johnstone & Rivera, as cited in Darken wald & Merriam, 1982). Mental age is assessed by comparing scores achieved in intelligence or achievement tests. In such cases, standard scores have already been set for different chronological ages (The American Medical Association, 1989). Those in psychological testing, therefore, set sixteen as the chronological age for adults, mainly because the WAIS III (Wechsler Adult Intelligence Scale, Third Revision) begins its adult testing at age sixteen. Also, Roger Gould's (1978) adult developmental stage begins at sixteen. Neuroandragogy however, suggests a higher chronological age for the purpose of adult education after examining physical, mental and developmental arguments. Neuroandragogy views the age of twenty or older as the most appropriate because the brain has not reached maturity until at least age twenty, with further development in specific regions still occurring even into the fifth decade.

4. Adult Learning

Neuroandragogy acknowledges the cognitive functions and includes them all in adult learning. A definition for each is appropriate:

a. Learning must be defined in neurological terms.
    Solomon, Berg & Martin (1985) have defined learning as the involvement of storing information and then retrieving it, this depends on "synaptic plasticity, which involves complex biochemical processes, including actions of neurotransmitters and postsynaptic receptors" (p. 864). Learning must challenge and stimulate the adult brain without stress, causing growth of the central nervous system (Nussbaum, 2003).

b. Experience is an important learning tool for the adult student. Elbert, Heim & Rockstroh (2001) have concluded that "learning and experience affect the development of perceptual and cognitive abilities through mechanisms of reorganization of functional brain architecture, that is, through neural plasticity on a macroscopic scale" (p. 191).

c.   Memory is an important part of the learning process. It is defined as the retention of information and the "correspondence to patterns of chemical changes over the brain as a whole" (Russell, 1979, p. 144).

d.   Recall works with memory as a part of the learning process. The brain, according to Bransford et al. (1999), is actively at work both storing and recalling information. These cognitive functions have been found to operate differently in the brain of the adult than in the brain of the child.

Bearing these facts in mind, a working definition for adult learning would be defined as: The most relevant information passing through the cortex to the hippocampus where it is then stored. If this information finds other stored information in the brain it connects, if not it begins to make new memory. If used shortly after, this memory becomes permanent in the hippocampus and is pulled up by the cortex at the time of recall. If used daily or frequently enough it may remain in the cortex for quick references. This is made possible by the complex chemical interaction being performed at a high optimal level, releasing transmitters by special post and pre-synaptic receptors. This in turn forms new synaptic connections. The retrieval of the stored information is a timely and slow process, performed by the neurocortex. If pressured the recall is even slower or impossible at the time most needed.

5. Adult Brain Differences

As soon as brain development begins anatomical and physiological changes begin to occur. Some researchers believe the changes that occur in the nervous system as we age may contribute to age related changes in cognitive performance (Lemme, 1999). Most of the literature on adult development presents the information of changes or differences as debilitating. This is true of the decrementalistic view of cognitive psychology. Neuroandragogy, however, sees brain development and brain differences between the adult and the child as a positive change. It sees the child's brain as having potential for continual growth, and the adult's brain as being mature, filled with wisdom and experience, with room for further development (plasticity).

The following anatomical differences do not infer decline in mental functions and cognitive abilities: (a) As the brain ages the thickness of the cortex shrinks from 4.0mm in the eighteen-year-old to 3.12mm in the eighty-two-year-old; (b) there is a gradual loss of nerve cells, dendrites and synapses; (c) there is loss of neurons especially in the frontal lobe; (d) atrophy in prefrontal cortex; (e) progressive damage to the hippocampus; (f) brain weight and volume steadily declines. While some adults age gracefully, others may decline considerably, however, neuroandragogy holds that these anatomical changes do not prevent learning (Andreasen, 2001; Lemme, 1999) nor do they prevent neural plasticity or neurogenesis.

6. Differences in the Learning Process

Neuroandragogy concludes that because the adult brain shows a difference in development when compared with the child, the learning processes are expected to be different. Fisher & Rose (1998) agree that adults reason at a higher level than children because life experiences force this level of learning; brain receptors may also be responsible for higher learning levels. According to German researcher Sakman (Bass, 1998), a receptor within the brain is responsible for higher brain functions. The adult also processes information differently, usually slowing with age; thus the adult needs adequate time for learning to take place (Gregory, ed. 1998; Restak, 2001). The central theory of neuroandragogy proposes that learning for adults is possible, and different from that of children.

It is important that adult teachers recognize these differences because adults do not want to be treated like children who are still ruled by their emotions. Adults must be reasoned with and given equal opportunities to be rational in the learning experience.

7. The Positive Effects of Education on the Biological and Physiological Functions of the Adult Brain

Neuroandragogy acknowledges the great benefits for the adult who seeks lifelong education as a part of life. Research has proven that increased scores on fluid intelligence tests (Baltes, 1998), increase in brain plasticity and brain cell growth (Andreasen, 2001) result from educational intervention. Empirical tests on adult mice given enriched living conditions concluded that they grew sixty percent more new neurons and performed better on learning tests (Myers, 2003). The same results are now being reported by scientists for educated adults fifty to seventy years of age. This growth is found in the hippocampus and olfactory bulb regions (Carper, 2000). Andreasen has added that education not only grows brain cells but that it also lessens the risk of adults developing brain dementia. Nussbaum (2003) sees adult education as a healthy mental exercise for the brain.

8. Why Age-Related Physical Changes Do Not Dictate Decrease in Brain Plasticity

Neuroandragogy upholds research that the brain plasticity of the aging adult is not necessarily affected as long as the adult keeps using the brain correctly. Rybash, Roodin & Santrock (1991) found that despite biological age related changes, there was still a great deal of brain plasticity in adult intelligence. Restak (2001) believes loss of plasticity is a result of expectation and misuse of the brain. However, if the "use it or lose it" model is taken seriously by the aging adult, plasticity remains possible.

9. Testing and the Adult Brain

Researchers in adult education have concluded that intelligence tests, with emphasis on cognitive skills and formal logic, are no longer considered appropriate for all adult life situations (Tennant & Pogson, 1995). Also, adults have been found to perform poorly on timed tests. Gregory (ed., 1998) believes the adult's brain becomes hidebound or inflexible if placed under pressure to respond to any learning situation. Neuroandragogy emphasizes that adult students are more likely to experience timed test anxiety than their youth counterparts. However, they will do just as well if not timed or placed under pressure.

Teachers of adults, policy makers, administrators etc. must begin to seek new ways to evaluate adult students outside of timed testing. Adults should not be measured in this way, but must be judged on their own merits, their own capabilities, and in their own timing. Open book test, take home exams, timeless class room test, projects, papers etc. are effective ways used to evaluate adults.

10. The Adult Educator

Adult educators should 1) teach with as much novelty as possible, for example: teach by way of controversy and in conflict to standard beliefs held by adult students; 2) Employ activities or teaching practices that involve all five senses to heighten memory and recall possibilities (Marieb, 1999; Hansome, 1931, Solomon, Breg & Martin, 1999).

a. Adult educators must depart from decrementalistic views of inevitable decline often found in studies of psychology and give their students hope by promoting a continued potential view that acknowledges compensation for loss (Lemme, 1999).

b. Adult educators must reevaluate old theories regarding adults, their education and learning. They must begin to show interest in understanding current research regarding adults, including brain sciences, as this will contribute to improved professional practice (Bruer, 1999; Sousa, 1998).

c. Adult educators must involve students in designing curriculums that encourage complexity, novelty and creativity according to the interest of the adult student, and the scope of their experience and expertise (Knowles, 1990; Tennant & Pogson, 1995). However, each educator must bear in mind that what's complex to one student is not to the other. Thus variety is important.

d. Adult educators must teach students to learn how to memorize, how to store information and how to recall it upon demand (Bruer, 1999; Fisher & Rose, 1998).

e. Adult educators must lead students through the process of unlearning; this helps to eliminate old ideas making room for new ones, especially new information regarding their neural development and learning abilities (Bruer, 1999; Rosenstock in Hansome, 1931).

11. Adult Education

a. Adult education must help students unlearn old ideas and myths about the brain. There must be more effort made to teach how the brain learns and the many benefits of new learning. (Bruer, 1999; Rosenstock in Hansome, 1931).

b. Adult education should not be approached or presented as a means to an end (job promotion, degree, etc.), but must be presented as an instrument of improvement for ones-self and the community at large. It must also be presented as an instrument capable of improving brain health.

c. Adult education must in itself be promoted as a health tool. It is time to recognize education as a discipline that contributes to the well being of the individual. The brain must be recognized as being a critical part of the body and education must be used to maximize its capacity and sustain its health (Nussbaum, 2003).

d. Adult education must encourage a proactive lifestyle among adults involving novelty, creativity and complexity. Adult education must encourage adult students to seek a life style that will improve their chance for longer life, better brain health and memory improvement. Exercise and nutrition programs should become a part of all adult education programs.

e. Adult education should always make available new research regarding the brain and learning, to improve an awareness of the neurosciences.

f. Adult education must be highlighted as a preventable measure against some neurodegenerative disorders.

g. Adult education must create enriched learning environments to include: mental stimulation, socialization, and physical activity.

APPENDIX

SAMPLES OF FIRST WORKS IN ANDRAGOGY

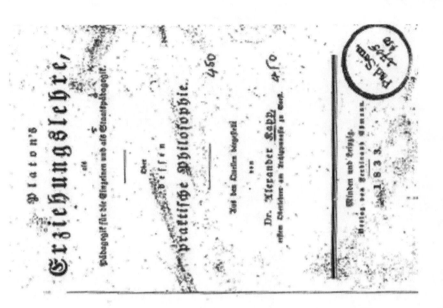

HERAUSGEBER:

A. FISCHER ❖ W. FLITNER ❖ TH. LITT ❖ H. NOHL E. SPRANGER

4. JAHRG. / HEFT 6   LEIPZIG   MÄRZ 1929

*   I N H A L T   *

Und es darf uns natürlich nicht hindern, die alten Wissensgebiete heranzuziehen, die bisher unsere Lehren schon mittelbar mit betreut haben. In unserem Werk: „Im Kampf um die Erwachsenenbildung" haben Picht und ich 1926 durch unser Kapitel „Andragogik" die Pädagogik aus ihrer Vereinzelung herauszulösen versucht. Aber nicht nur die Pädagogik hat vorgearbeitet. Die neue Grundwissenschaft wird nämlich einerseits vieles von dem benutzen müssen, was die Großen der Pädagogik immer gelehrt

FRANZ PÖGGELER

1957

Einführung
in die Andragogik

Grundfragen der Erwachsenenbildung

A. HENN VERLAG · RATINGEN B. DÜSSELDORF

235

REFERENCES

Achtemeier, P., Green, J. B., & Thompson, M. M. (2001). *Introducing the New Testament, its literature and theology.* Grand Rapids: W. B. Eerdmans.

American Heritage Dictionary (2000). Boston: Houghton Mifflan.

American Medical Association: Encyclopedia of medicine (1989). New York, Random House.

Anderson, M., & Lindeman, E. C. (1927). *Education through experience.* New York: The Workers Education Bureau Press.

Andreasen, N. C. (1984). *The broken brain: The biological revolution in psychiatry.* New York: Harper and Row.

Andreasen, N. C. (2001). *Brave new brain.* New York: Oxford University Press.

Andrews, T. E., Houston, W. R., & Bryant, B. L. (1981). *Adult learners.* Washington, D.C.: Association of Teacher Educators.

Ardagh, J. (1995). *Germany and the Germans.* England: Penguin Books (Original work published 1961).

Ary, D., Jacobs, L. C., & Razavieh, A. (1990). *Introduction to research in education.* Fort Worth: Holt, Rinehart and Winston.

Balota, D. A., Dolan, P. O., & Duchek, J. M. (2000). Memory changes in healthy older adults. In E. Tulving and F. I. M. Craik (Eds.), *Oxford Handbook of Memory.* Oxford University Press.

Baltes, P. B. (1998). Theoretical propositions of life-span developmental psychology: On the dynamics between growth and decline. In M. P. Lawton and T. A. Salthouse (1998) *Essential papers on the psychology of aging.* New York: New York University Press.

Baltes, P. B., Kliegl, R., & Dittman-Kohli, F. (1988). On the locus of training gains in research on the plasticity of fluid intelligence in old age. *Journal of Educational Psychology,* 80 (N3), 392–400.

Baltes, P. B., & Mayer, K. U. (Ed.). (1999). *The Berlin aging study: Aging from 70 to 100.* Berlin, Germany: Berlin-Brandenburg Academy of Sciences.

Baltes, P. B., Sawarka, D., & Kliegl, R. (1989). Cognitive training research on fluid intelligence in old age: What can older adults achieve by themselves? *Psychology and Aging, 4* (N4), 217–221.

Baltes, P. B., & Schaie, K. W. (1973). *Life-span developmental psychology: Personality and socialization.* New York: Academic Press.

Barclay, W. (1961). *The mind of Jesus.* San Francisco: Harper Collins.

Barnard, H. (1964). The American lyceum, *American Journal of Education,* in C. O. Houle (1992). *The Literature of Adult Education, A Bibliographic Essay.* California: Jossey-Bass.

Barzun, J., & Graff, H. F. (1957). *The modern researcher.* New York: Harcourt, Brace & World.

Bass, T. (1994) *Reinventing the future: Conversations with the world's leading scientists.* Reading: Massachusetts: Addison-Weeley.

Beaman, R. (1998). The unquiet...even loud andragogy! Alternative assessments for adult learners. *Innovative Higher Education, 23* (1), 47–59.

Beder, H. W., & Darkenwald, G. G. (1982). Differences between teaching adults and pre-adults: Some Propositions and Findings. *Adult Education, 32* (N8), 142–155.

Belanger, P. (1993). Germany. *Rethinking adult education for development* (1st ed.). Ljubljana, Slovenia: Slovenia Ministry of Science & Technology.

Bell, C. R. (1989). Malcolm. *Training and Development Journal,* 40–43.

Belsky, J. (1984). *The psychology of aging theory, research and practice.* Monterey: Brooks/Cole.

Bereday, G. Z. F. (1964). *Comparative method in education.* Holt, Rinehart and Winston.

Berger, K. S. (1993). *The developing person through the life span.* Worth Publishers.

Best, J. W., & Kahn, J. V. (1998). *Research in education.* New Jersey: Prentice Hall.

Billington, D. D. (2000). Seven characteristics of highly effective adult learning programs. *The adult learner in higher education and the workplace.* http://www.newhorizons.org

Birren, J. E. (1964). *The psychology of aging.* New Jersey: Prentice-Hall.

Birren, J. E. (1977). As cited in Terry, E. F. (1988) Using andragogy to foster moral development of adults within the institutional church. *Lifelong Learning: An Omnibus of Practice and Research, 12 (N2).*

Birren, J. E., & Schaie, K. W. (1985). *Handbook of the Psychology of Aging* (2nd ed.).

Black, S. (1997). Late lessons. *The American School Board Journal,* 40–42.

Blanchard-Fields, F., & Hess, T. M. (1996). *Perspectives on cognitive change in adulthood and aging.* New York: McGraw-Hill.

Bloom, F. E., & Lazerson, A. (1988). Brain, mind, and behavior. New York: W. H. Freeman.

Bloom, F. E., Beal. F. & Kupfer, D. (2003). *The DANA guide to brain health.* New York: The DANA Press.

Boeren, A. (1993). The Netherlands: *Rethinking adult education for development* (1st ed.). Ljubljana, Slovenia: Slovenia Ministry of Science and Technology.

Bogdan, R., & Biklen, S. K. (1982). *Qualitative research for education to theory and methods.* Boston: Allyn and Bacon.

Borg, W., & Gall, M. D. (1983). *Educational research.* New York: Longman.

Botwinick, J. (1984). *Aging and behavior: A comprehension integration of research findings.* New York: Springer.

Boyd, D. R., & Apps, W. J. and Associates (1984). Redefining the discipline of adult education. Dusan Savicevic, Contemporary trends in adult education research in Yugoslavia *International Journal of Lifelong Education,* 9 (N2), 129–135.

Bransford, J. D., Brown, A. L., & Cocking, R. R. (1999). *How people learn.* Washington, D. C.: National Academy Press.

Brookfield, S. D. (1984). The Contribution of Eduard Lindeman To The Development of Theory and Philosophy in Adult Education. *Adult Education Quarterly, 34* (N4), 185–196.

Brookfield, S. D. (1987). *Understanding and facilitating adult learning.* San Fran cisco: Jossey-Bass.

Bruer, J. T. (1999). In search of Brain-based education. *Phi Delta Kappa*: 649–657.

Bugelski, B. R. (1973). 'Human Learning' in Handbook of General Psychology, Benjamin B. Walman (Ed), New Jersey: Prentice-Hall.

Burger, J. F. (1926). *Verglihende Untersuchengen Uber die Volkschochschulbewe gung in Danemark, England Deutschland.* Munich: Universitet.

Buzan, T. (1994). *The mind map book.* London: Penguin Books.

Caine, G., & Caine, R. N. (1995). Reinventing schools through Brain-based learning. *Educational Leadership, 52* (N2), 101–105.

Caine, G., & Caine, R. N. (1997). *Education on the edge of possibility.* Alexandria: ASCD.

Calman, A. M. (2001). *Oxford Dictionary of Psychology.* Oxford University Press.

Carlson, R. A. (1979). The time of andragogy. *Adult Education,* 30, 53–56.

Carlson, R. A. (1989). Malcolm Knowles: Apostle of andragogy. *Vitae Scholasticae, 8* (NI), 217–233.

Carmichael, M. (2002, February 18). New cells in the thinking cap? Think again. *Newsweek*, p. 12.

Carper, J. (2000). *Your miracle brain.* New York: Quill.

Carter, R. (1998). *Mapping The Mind.* Berkeley: University of California Press.

Cassara, B. (1993). America. *Rethinking adult education for development* (1st ed.). Ljubljana, Slovenia: Slovenia Ministry of Science & Technology.

Cervero, R. (1993). America. *Rethinking adult education for development* (1st ed.). Ljubljana, Slovenia: Slovenia Ministry of Science & Technology.

Challis, (1996). Andragogy and the accreditation of prior learning: points on a continuum or uneasy bedfellows? *International Journal of Lifelong Educa tion, 15* (NI), 32–40.

Chamberland, E. (Ed.). (1995). *L'andragogie histoire, défis, prospective.* Université De Montréal (L. Bollinger, Trans.).

Charters, A. N. (1993). America. *Rethinking adult education for development* (1st ed.). Ljubljana, Slovenia: Slovenia Ministry of Science & Technology.

Charters, A. N. (1995). *Methods of comparative andragogy: An international expert seminar.* Bamberg, Germany.

Charters, A. N. (1999). Standards for Comparative Adult Education Research. In J. Reischman, M. Bron, & Z. Jelenc (Ed.), Comparative Adult Education 1998. The contribution of ISCAE to an Emerging Field of Study. International Society for Comparative Adult Education, Bamberg, Germany.

Classroom Compass (1995), 1 (N3). *Constructing Knowledge in the Classroom.*

Clayman, C. B. (Ed.). (1989). *The American Medical Association Encyclopedia of Medicine.* New York: Random House.

Collinson, D., & Wilkinson, R. (1994). *Thirty-Five oriental philosophers.* Lon don: Routledge.

Cooke, J. C. (1994). *Malcolm Shepherd Knowles, the father of American andragogy: A biographical study*. Unpublished doctoral dissertation, University of North Texas, Texas.

Courtenay, B., & Stevenson, R. (1983). Avoiding the threat of gogymania. *Life long Learning: The Adult Years*, 10–11.

Creswell, J. W. (1998). *Research design: qualitative & quantitative approaches*. Thousand Oaks, CA: Sage.

Cropley, A. J. (1998). Lifelong Education: Research Strategies. In *Lifelong education for adults: An International Handbook*. C. J. Titmus (Ed.). Oxford: Pergamon Press.

Cross, K. P. (1984). *Adults as learners: increasing participation and facilitating learning*. San Francisco: Jossey-Bass Publishers.

D'Arcangelo, M. (1998a). *An Interview with Robert Sylvester*. Adopted from the Brain and Learning Video Tape, Alexandra, VA: ASCD.

D'Arcangelo, M. (1998b). The brains behind the brain. *Educational Leadership*. 20–25.

Dailey, N. (1984). Adult learning and organizations. *Training and Development Journal*.

Darkenwald, G. G., & Merriam, S. B. (1982). *Adult education: Foundations of practice*, New York: Harper and Row.

Davenport, J. (1984). Adult educators and andragogical pedagogical orientations: A review of the literature. *MPAEA Journal*, 8–17.

Davenport, J. (1987). Is there any way out of the andragogy morass? *Lifelong learning: An omnibus of practice and research, 11* (N3), 17–20.

Davenport, J., & Davenport, J. (1984). A chronology and analysis of the andragogy debate. *Adult Education Quarterly, 35* (N1), 152–159.

Dawson, R. (1981). *Confucius and Chinese humanism*. New York: Funk & Wag nalls.

Denzin, N. K., & Lincoln, Y. S. (1998). *The landscape of qualitative research: theories & issues.* Thousand Oaks, CA: Sage.

Diamond, M. (1988). *Enriching heredity.* The Free Press: Simon and Schuster.

Diamond, M. (1997). The significance of enrichment. *The Brain Lab.* Seattle, WA: New Horizons for Learning.

Diamond, M. (1998). *Older brains new connections:* A *conversation with Marion Diamond at 73.* Davidson Films.

Dibbits, T., & van Essenberg, A. (1978), et al (Eds), *Sociale pedagogiek.* Amster dam/Meppel: Boon.

Dinmore, I. (1997). Interdisciplinary and integrative learning: An imperative for adult education. *Education: Chula Vista, 117* (N3), 452–467.

Dittmann-Kohli, F. (1981). Learning how to learn: A psychological approach to self directed learning. *Education, 24,* 23–33.

Dohmen, G. (1993). America. *Rethinking adult education for development* (1st ed.). Ljubljana, Slovenia: Slovenia Ministry of Science & Technology.

Dowling, J. E. (1992). *Neurons and networks: An introduction to neuroscience.* Cambridge: The Belknap Press of Harvard University Press.

Draper, J. A. (1998, May 1). The metamorphoses of andragogy. *Cjsae/Rcééa 12.*

Ebner, F. F. (1996). Teaching the brain to learn. *Peabody Journal of Education, 71* (4), 143–151.

Edgell, D., & William, G. (1993). *Learning disabilities and brain function: A neuropsychological approach.* New York: Springer-Verlog.

Elbert, T., Heim, S., & Rockstroh, B. (2001). Neural plasticity and develop ment. *The Handbook of Developmental Cognitive Neuroscience,* C. A. Nelson and M. Luciana (Ed.), Cambridge: MIT Press

Elias, J. L. (1979). Andragogy revisited. *Adult Education, 29* (4), 252–256.

Elias, J. L., & Merriam, S. (1980). *Philosophical foundations of adult education.* Florida, Malabar: Robert E. Krieger.

Elias, M. F., Elias, P. K., & Elias, J. W. (1977). *Basic processes in adult develop mental psychology*. St. Louis: The C. V. Mosby Co.

Engelhart, M. D. (1972). *Methods of educational research*. Chicago: Rand McNally.

Farmer, J. A. (1993). America. *Rethinking adult education for development* (1st ed.). Ljubljana, Slovenia: Slovenia Ministry of Science & Technology.

Faure, E., Herrera, F., Kaddowra, A., Lopes, H., Petrovsky, A. V., Rahnema, M. and Ward, F. C. (1972). *Learning to be: The World of education today and tomorrow*. Harrap, London: Uesco Paris.

Ferguson, M. (1973). *The brain revolution: The* frontiers *of mind research*. New York: Toplinger.

Ferro, T. R. (1997). *The linguistics of andragogy and its offspring*. John Henschke, Historical Antecedents shaping conceptions of Andragogy: A Comparison of Sources and Roots. Radouljica, Slovenia. (Unpublished manuscript)

Fessard, A., Gerarad, R. W., Konorski, J. (1961). *Brain mechanisms and learning: A symposium organized by the council for international organizations of medi cal sciences established under the joint auspices of UNESCO and World Health Organization*. Blackwell Scientific Publications Oxford.

Feuer, D., & Geber, B. (1988). Uh-oh…second thoughts about adult learning theory. *Training*, 31–39.

Finch, C. (2003). In Guttman, M., The aging brain. [Disk].

File://A:/The_Aging_Brain.htm.

Finger, S. (1994). Origins of neuroscience: *A History of Explorations into Brain Function*. New York, Oxford University Press.

Finger, S. (2000). *Minds behind the brain*. Oxford: Oxford University Press.

Fischer, K. W., & Rose, S. P. (1998, November). Growth cycles of brain and mind. *Educational Leadership*. 56–60.

Fisher, J. C., & Podeschi, R. L. (1989). From Lindeman to Knowles: A change in vision. P. Jarvis and J. E. Thomas, *International Journal of Lifelong Educ tion*. London: Taylor and Francis.

Fogarty, R. (1997). *Brain-compatible classrooms*. Arlington Heights: Skylight Professional Development.

Fogiel, M. (1999). *REA's solver's psychology*. New Jersey: Research and Education Association.

Fogiel, M. (2000). *Psychology one*. Research and Education Association.

Frick, E. (1989). Theories of learning and their impact on OPAC instructions. *Research Strategies*.

Friedenthal-Haase, M. (1993). Germany. *Rethinking adult education for development* (1st ed.). Ljubljana, Slovenia: Slovenia Ministry of Science & Technology.

Friedenthal-Haase, M. (Ed.). (1998). *Personality and conference on the history of biography: Proceedings of the sixth international adult education, Vol. I: Gen eral, comparative*, and *synthetic studies*. Europäischer Verlag der Wissen schaften: Peter Lang.

Friedenthal-Haase, M. (Ed.). (1998). *Personality and biography: Proceedings of the sixth international conference on the history of adult education, Vol. II: Biogra phies of adult educators from five continents*. Europäischer Verlag der Wissen schaften: Peter Lang.

Friedenthal-Haase, M., Hake, B. J., & Marriate, S. (Eds.) (1991). *British-Dutch-German relationships in adult education 1880–1930*. Leeds studies in con tinuing education cross-cultural studies in the education of adults, number 1.

Furter, P. (1971). Grandeur et misère de la Pédagogie. University of Neuchâtel. (From, Fawre, E., Herrera, F., Kaddoura, A., Lopes, H., Petrovsky, A., Rahnema, M., & Ward, F. E. (1972). *Learning to be*. Paris: UNESCO).

Gaddes, W. H., & Edgell, D. (1994). *Learning disabilities and brain function*. New York: Springer-Verlag.

Galfo, A., & Miller, C. E. (1965). *Interpreting education research*. Dubuque, IA: W. C. Brown.

Gardener, H. (1983). *Frames of mind*. New York: Basic Books.

Gardner, H. (1993). *Multiple Intelligences*. New York: Basic Books.

Gardner, H. (1999). *Intelligence reframed: Multiple intelligences for the 21st century*. New York: Basic Books.

Gay, L. R. (1981). *Educational research: competencies for analysis and application*. Columbus: C. E. Merrill.

Gay, L. R. (1995). *Educational evaluation and measurement: competencies for analysis and application*. Columbus: C. E. Merrill.

Gerow, J. R. (1992). *Psychology: an introduction*, (3rd ed.). Indiana: Harper Collins.

Giczkowski, W. (1998). General education applications for adult learners: Making sense of experience. *Adult Learning, 9* (N4), 30–32.

Giuld, P. B., & Garger, S. (1998). *Marching to different drummers* (2nd ed.). Alexandria, VA: ASCD.

Goleman, D. (1995). *Emotional intelligence: Why it can matter more than IQ*. New York: Bantam Books.

Good, C. V. (1966). *Educational research: methodology and design*. New York: Appleton-Century-Crofts.

Gottfredson, L. (1999). *The Scientific American book of the brain*. Connecticut: The Lyons Press.

Gould, R. (1978). Transformations. In W. Weiten and M. A. Lloyd (1994), *Psychology applied to modern life*. Pacific Grove, CA: Brooks/Cole.

Gould, R. L. (1978). *Transformations: growth and change in adult life*. New York: Simon and Schuster.

Grace, A. P. (1996). Striking a critical pose: andragogy-missing links, missing values. *International Journal of Lifelong Education, 15* (5), 382–392.

Greenfield, S. (2000). *Brain story: Unlocking our inner world of emotions, memories, ideas, and desires.* London: BBC Worldwide Limited.

Greenspan, S. I. (1997). *The growth of the mind.* Massachusetts: Pereus Books.

Gregory, R. L. (Ed.). (1998). *The Oxford companion to the mind.* Oxford: Oxford University Press.

Griffith, S., & Mclusky, H. Y. (Eds.) (1981). *The AEA handbook series in adult education.* San Francisco: Jossey-Bass.

Gross, C. G. (1998). *Brain vision memory.* Cambridge, Massachusetts: The M.I.T. Press.

Gross, R. (Ed.). (1982) *Invitation to lifelong learning.* Chicago: Follett.

Guilford, J. P. (1973). Theories of intelligence. *Handbook of General Psychology,* Benjamin B. Walman (Ed), New Jersey: Prentice-Hall.

Gutek, G. L. (1995). *A history of the western educational experience* (2nd ed.). Prospect Heights: Waveland Press.

Guttman, M. (2003). The Aging Brain. [Disk]. File://A:\The_Aging_Brian.htm.

Guyton, A. G., & Hall, J. E. (2000). *The text book of medical physiology.* Philadelphia: W. B. Saunders.

Hake, B. J. (1999). Problems and pitfalls in comparative andragogy: Some notes on the research process in comparative historical studies: *Comparative Adult Education 1998. The Contribution of ISCAE to an Emerging Field of Study.* Slovenia Ministry of Science & Technology, Ljubljana.

Hall, E. F. (1998). *Pedagogical and andragogical principles of John Wesley's anthology.* Unpublished doctoral dissertation, University of North Texas, Texas.

Hammink, K. (1993). The Netherlands: *Rethinking adult education for development* (1st ed.). Ljubljana, Slovenia: Slovenia Ministry of Science and Technology.

Hansome, M. (1931). *World worker's educational movements: Their social significance.* (Doctoral dissertation, Columbia University, 1931). New York.

Harris, W. J. A. (1980). *Comparative adult education: Practice, purpose and theory.* London: Longman.

Hartree. A. (1984). Malcolm Knowles' theory of andragogy: A critique. *International Journal of Lifelong Education, 3* (N3), 203–210.

Have, T. T. (1971). *Andragogie.* Amsterdam.

Hebb, D. O. (1949). *The organization of behavior: A neuropsychological theory.* New York: John Wiley & Sons.

Heidemann,   G.   (2003).   The   amazing   brain.   [Disk].   File:// A:\The_Amazing_Brain.htm.

Hellyer, M. (1990). Uncovering the untold story of the history of adult education in the United States: Implications of the labor college movement. Franz Pöggeler (Ed.). *The State and Adult Education: Historical and System atical Aspects.* Frankfurtam Main, Germany: Verlog Peter Lang.

Henschke, J. A. (1993). America. *Rethinking adult education for development* (1st ed.). Ljubljana, Slovenia: Slovenia Ministry of Science & Technology.

Henschke, J. A. (1995). *Theory and practice on preparing human resource develop ment professionals.* Academy of human resource development, 1995 conference proceedings, University of Missouri: St. Louis.

Henschke, J. A. (1997/1998). In memoriam: Malcolm S. Knowles. *Adult Learn ing, 9* (N2), 2–4.

Henschke, J. A. (1998a). *Historical antecedents shaping conceptions of andragogy: A comparison of sources and roots.* Paper presented at the International Confer ence on Research in Comparative Andragogy, Radiovjica, Slovenia.

Henschke, J. A. (1998b). Modeling the preparation of adult educators. *Adult Learning.*

Henstrom, R. (1993). America. *Rethinking adult education for development* (1st ed.). Ljubljana, Slovenia: Slovenia Ministry of Science & Technology.

Hiemstra, R. (1993). America. *Rethinking adult education for development* (1st ed.). Ljubljana, Slovenia: Slovenia Ministry of Science & Technology.

Hiemstra, R., & Sisco, B. (1990). *Individualizing instruction.* San Francisco: Jossey-Bass.

Hill, W. F. (1990). *Learning: A survey of psychological interpretations.* New York: Harper and Row.

Honzik, M. P. (1973). The Development of Intelligence. *Handbook of General Psychology,* Benjamin B. Walman (Ed.), New Jersey: Prentice-Hall.

Horn, J. (1998). In Woodruff-Pak, D. S., Psychology and *aging.* Englewood Cliffs, NJ: Prentice Hall.

Horn, J. L. & Cattell, R. B. (1997). In Woodruff-Pak, D. S., *Psychology and aging.* Englewood Cliffs, NJ: Prentice Hall.

Horn, J. L. & Cattell, R. B. Age differences in fluid and crystallized intelligence. In M. P. Lawton and T. A. Salthouse (1998) *Essential papers on the psychology of aging.* New York, New York University.

Houle, C. O. (1993). America. *Rethinking adult education for development* (1st ed.). Ljubljana, Slovenia: Slovenia Ministry of Science & Technology.

How can research on the brain inform education (1997). *Classroom Compass, 3* (N2), 1–8. http://www.sedl.org/scimath/ compass/vo3no2/brain.html.

Howard, P. J. (2000). *The owner's manual for the brain,* (2nd ed.). Austin: Bard Press.

Howe, C. O. (1992). *The literature of adult education a bibliography.* California: Jossey-Bass.

Hudson, J. W. (1969). *The history of adult education.* New York: Augustus M. Kelly.

Hyland, K. P. (2001). New neurons in brain shown to help form new memories. UniSci-Daily University Science News. Webmaster@unisci.com.

Imel, S. (1989). Teaching adults: Is it different? *Eric Digest No. 82,* 1–4.

Isaacs, J., & Downing, T. (1998). *Cold War.* Canada: Little, Brown and Company.

Ivan, S. (1986, July). *Toward a typology of European adult education historiogr phy.* Paper presented at the international conference on the history of adult education, Oxford, England.

J. A. Comenius, Selected Pedagogical Works (1982). Vol. 2. Moscow: Pedagogica.

Jacks, L. P. (1931). *The education of the whole man.* New York: Harper & Broth ers.

Jackson, C. L., & DuVall, L. A. (1989, May). *Designing programs for adults–Let's not overlook andragogy.* Paper presented at annual conference on nontraditional/ interdisciplinary programs, Virginia Beach, VA.

Jarvis, P. (1981) The open university unit: Andragogy or pedagogy? *Teaching at a Distance 20,* 24–29.

Jarvis, P. (1987a) Meaningful and meaningless experience: Towards an analysis of learning from life. *Adult Education Quarterly, 37* (N3), 164–172.

Jarvis, P. (Ed.). (1987b). *Twentieth century thinkers in adult education.* London: Croom Helm.

Jarvis, P. (1992). Towards a Comparative Analysis? In P. Jarvis, Perspectives on Adult Education and Training in Europe. Edinburgh, England: The National Institute of Adult Continuing Education.

Jarvis, P. (1993). *Adult education and the state.* London: Routledge.

Jarvis, P., Halford, J., & Griffin, C. (1998). *The theory and practice of learning.* London: Kogan Page.

Jarvis, P., & Pöggeler, F. (Eds.) (1994). *Developments in the education of adults in Europe.* Europäischer Verlag Der Wissenschaften: Peter Lang.

Jeffus, D. (2003). Personal conversation. Hillcrest Medical Center, Tulsa, OK.

Jensen, E. (1995). *The learning brain.* San Diego: Turning Point.

Johnson, B., & Christensen, L. (2000). *Educational research: quantitative and qualitative approaches.* Boston: Allyn and Bacon.

Jourdan, M., (Ed.). (1981). *Recurrent education in Western Europe.* NFER-Nel son.

Jug, J., & Pöggeler, F. (Eds.) (1996). *Democracy and adult education.* Europäis cher Verlag Der Wissenschaften: Peter Lang.

Kaos, J. H., & Florence, S. L. (1996). Brain reorganization and experience. *Pea body of Journal of Education, 71* (4), 152–167.

Kapp, A. (1833). *Platon's Erziehungslehre, als pádagogik für die linzelnen und als ctaatspádagogik.* Minden und Leipzig. Berlog Von Ferbinanb Grmann.

Karmos, J. S., & Greathouse, L. (1989). Teaching adults myths and principles. *Vocational Education Journal,* 28–29.

Katus, J., & Toth, J. (Eds.) (1985). On adult education and public information in Hungary and the Netherlands. Paper presented at the Hungarian-Dutch Symposium on Adult Education and Public Information.

Katz, E. (1976). *The belief In andragogy and the development of self-actualization.* (Doctoral dissertation, Boston University).

Kausler, D. H. (1991). *Experimental psychology, cognition, and human aging.* (2nd ed.). New York: Springer-Verlag.

Kazemek, F. E., & Rigg, P. (1983). *Treating men like boys; Pedagogy at a job corps center.* Carbondale: Southern Illinois University Press.

Khachaturian, Z. S. (2000). In Peck, P., Age and Dementia Don't Have to Go Hand in Hand (On-line). Available: http://my.webmd. com/content/article/ 26/1728_59434.

Kincheloe, J. L., Steinberg, S. R., & Villaverde, L. E. (1999). *Rethinking intelli- gence.* New York: Routledge.

Kliegl, R., Smith, J, & Baltes, P. B. (1989). Testing the limits and the study of adult age differences in cognitive plasticity of a mnemonic skill. *Develop- mental Psychology, 25* (N2).

Kline, P. (1998). *The new psychometrics.* London: Routledge.

Knoll, J. (1981a). Federal Republic of Germany: Training adult educators in the federal republic and the German Democratic Republic. M. Jourdan (Ed.), *Recurrent education in Western Europe: Progress, projects and trends in recurrent, lifelong and continuing education.* The NFER: Nelson.

Knoll, J. (1981b). Professionalization in adult education in the Federal Republic of Germany and the German Democratic Republic. W. S. Griffith and H. U. McClusky (Ed.), *Comparing adult education worldwide.* San Francisco: Jossey-Bass.

Knoll, J. (1993). Germany. *Rethinking adult education for development.* 1st ed. Ljubljana, Slovenia: Slovenia Ministry of Science & Technology.

Knowles, M. S. (1970). *Modern practice of adult education: Andragogy versus pedagogy.* New York: Association Press.

Knowles, M. S. (1973). *The adult learner: A neglected species.* Houston, TX: Gulf.

Knowles, M. S. (1979). Andragogy revisited part II. *Adult Education, 30,* 52–53.

Knowles, M. S. (1982). Andragogy: The new science of education, R. Gross (Ed.) 1982, *Invitation to Lifelong Learning.* Chicago: Follett.

Knowles, M. S. (1984). *Andragogy in action.* San Francisco: Jossey-Bass.

Knowles, M. S. (1990). *The adult learner: A neglected species.* Houston: Gulf.

Knowles, M. S. (1993). America. *Rethinking adult education for development,* 1st ed. Slovenia Ministry of Science & Technology, Ljubljana.

Knowles, M. S. (1996). Adult learning. in Craig, R. L., (ed). ASTD Training and Development Handbook: A Guide to Human Resource Development, Fourth Edition, New York: McGRaw Hill.

Knox, A. B. (1989). Adult education. Research: United States. Colin J. Titmus (Ed.), *Lifelong Education for Adults,* University of Leeds, U.K.: Pergamon Press.

Knox, A. B. (Ed.). (1991). *The Jossey-Bass higher adult education series.* San Francisco: Jossey-Bass.

Knox, A. B. (1992). *The literature of adult education: A bibliographic essay.* San Francisco: Jossey-Bass.

Knox, A. B. (1993). America. *Rethinking adult education for development.* 1st ed. Ljubljana, Slovenia: Slovenia Ministry of Science & Technology.

Knudsen, J. (Ed.). (1976). *Selected writings: N. F. S. Grundtvig.* Philadelphia: Fortress Press. (Knudson, J., Martensen, E., & Nielsen, E. D. trans.).

Knudsen R. (1978). 'Humanagogy anyone?' *Adult Education 29.*

Koepper, R. C. (1993). Germany. *Rethinking adult education for development.* 1st ed. Ljubljana, Slovenia: Slovenia Ministry of Science & Technology.

Kotulak, R. (1996). *Inside the brain: Revolutionary discoveries of how the mind works.* Kansas City, MO: Andrews and McMeel.

Krajnc, A. (1989). Andragogy. Colin J. Titmus (Ed.), *Lifelong Education for Adults.* University of Leeds, U.K. Pergamon Press.

Kuhn, T. S. (1964). In Pajares, F., *The structure of scientific revolutions* (On-line). Available: http://www.emory.edu/education/mfplkuhn.html. Outline and study guide, Emory University.

Lahey, B. B. (1998). *Psychology an introduction.* Boston: McGraw-Hill.

Lawton, M. P., & Salthouse, T. A. (1998). *Essential papers on the psychology of aging.* New York: New York University Press.

Lebel, J. (1978). *Beyond Andragogy to gerogogy. Lifelong learning: The adult years,* 16–25.

LeCompte, M. D., Millroy, W. L., & Preissle, J. (1992). *The handbook of qualitative research in education.* San Diego: Academic Press.

LeDoux, J. (2002). *Synaptic Self.* New York: Penguin Books.

Lemme, B. H. (1999). *Development in adulthood.* Boston: Allyn & Bacon.

Livecka, E. (1989). Adult education research: Eastern Europe and the Soviet Union. In Colin J. Titmus (Ed.), *Lifelong Education for Adults,* University of Leeds, U.K.: Pergamon Press.

LoBiondo-Wood, G., & Haber (1998). *Nursing research: methods, critical appraisal, and utilization.* St. Louis, MO: Mosby.

Lovell, R. B. (1980). *Adult learning.* London: Croom Helm.

Lund, R. D. (1978). *Development and plasticity of the brain: An introduction.* New York: Oxford University Press.

Lynch, G., & Wells, J. (1978). *Neuroanatomical plasticity and behavioral adaptability. Brain & Learning,* T. Teyler (Ed.). Stanford, CT: Greylock.

Marieb, E. N. (2001). *Human anatomy & physiology.* San Francisco: Benjamin Cummings.

Markowitsch, H. J. (2000). Neuroanatomy of memory. E. Tulving & F. I. M. Graik, *The Oxford handbook of memory.* Oxford, NY: Oxford University Press.

Markowitsch, H. J., & Kessler, J. (2000). Massive impairment in execution functions with partial presentation of other cognitive functions: the case of a young patient with severe degeneration of the prefrontal cortex (On-line). Available: http://link.springer.dellink/service/journals/200221/ contents/00100404/paper/500221000040

Marshak, R. J. (1983). What's between pedagogy and andragogy? *Training and Development Journal,* 80–81.

Mattaghy, F. M., Shah, N. J., Krause, B. J., Schmidt, D., Halsband, U., Jancke, L., & Müller-Gärtner, H. W. (1999). "Neuronal correlates of encoding and retrieval in episodic memory during a paired-word association learning task: a functional magnetic resonance imaging study" *Experimental brain research,* (3) v. 128, 332–342 (On-line). Available: Http://athene.em.springer.delegi/ viewhd.pl?/search97cgi/s97_cgi7action=view&vdkvgw

Mayer, F. (1967). *The great teachers.* New York: The Citadel Press.

McAdams, R. P. (1993). *Lessons from abroad: How other countries educate their children.* Pennsylvania, PA: Technomie.

McKenzie, L. (1997). The issue of andragogy. *Adult Education, 27,* 225–229.

McPherson, R. B., & Lorenz, J. A. (1985). The pedagogical and andragogical principal–the consummate teacher. *NASSP Bulletin*, 55–60.

Meltzoff, J. (1999). *Critical thinking about research*. Auburn Hill: Minnesota Data Reproductions Corp.

Merriam, S. B. (Ed.). (1993). *An update on adult learning theory*. San Francisco: Jossey-Bass.

Merriam, S. B. (1998). *Qualitative research and case study applications in educa tion*. San Francisco: Jossey-Bass.

Merriam, S. B., & Caffarella, R. S. (1991). *Learning in adulthood: A comprehensive guide*. San Francisco: Jossey-Bass.

Merriam, S. B., & Rosemary, S. C. (1991). "Learning in adulthood: A comprehensive guide," John Henschke, Historical Antecedents Shaping Concepts of Andragogy: A comparison of sources and roots. Radouljica, Slovenia.

Mezirow, J. (1991). *Transformative dimensions of adult learning*. San Francisco: Jossey-Bass.

Mezirow, J. (1993). America. *Rethinking adult education for development*. 1st ed. Ljubljana, Slovenia: Slovenia Ministry of Science & Technology.

Milligan, F. (1995). In defense of andragogy. *Nurse Education Today 15*, 22–27.

Misiak, H., & Sexton, V. S. (1966). *History of psychology: An overview*. New York: Grune & Stratton.

Möhle, H. (1990). Historical and contemporary aspects of the relationship between the state and the field of adult education in the German Democratic Republic. Franc Pöggeler (Ed.) *The state and adult education historical and systematical aspects*. Frankfurt am Main: Verlog Peter Lang.

Moore, A. B. (1993). America. *Rethinking adult education for development*. 1st ed. Ljubljana, Slovenia: Slovenia Ministry of Science & Technology.

Morris, J. C. (2000). In Peck, P., Age and Dementia Don't Have to Go Hand in Hand (On-line). Available: http://my.webmd.com/content/article/26/1728_59434.

Myers, R. (2002). *Neurorehabilitation in the twenty-*first *century.* (Lecture notes), Kaiser Rehabilitation Center, Tulsa, OK.

Neugarten, B. L. (Ed.). (1968). *Middle age and aging.* Chicago: The University of Chicago.

Newquist, H. P. (2004). *The great brain book.* China, Scholastic Reference.

Nixon-Ponder, S. (1995). *Eduard C. Lindeman in the field of adult education.* Kent State University, OH: Ohio Literacy Resource Center.

Nottingham Andragogy Group, The (1983). *Towards a developmental theory of andragogy.* University of Nottingham, England.

Numley, K. F. (2003). How the Adolescent Brain Challenges the Adult Brain (On-line). Available: http://help4teachers.com.

Nussbaum, P. D. (2003). *Brain Health and Wellness.* Tarentum, Pennsylvania: Word Association Publishers.

Nussbaum, P. D. (2004). Lifelong Learning and Wellness One Component to the Enlightened Gerosphere. Pnussbaum@lassenior.com.

On Purpose Associates. (2001). Brain-based learning (On-line). Available: http:// www.funderstanding.com/brain_based_learning.cfm.

On Purpose Associates. (2001). Neuroscience (On-line). Available: http:// www.funderstanding.com/neuroscience.cfm.

Parnell, D. (1996, March). Cerebral context. *Vocational Education Journal.*

Patton, M. Q. (1990). Qualitative evaluation and *research methods.* Newbury Park: CA.

Peers, R. (1926). Some applications of educational theory to adult education. *Adult Education, 1–11* (N1), 36–49.

Peers, R. (1934). *Adult education in practice.* London: MacMillan.

Pirtle, W. G. (1966). The history of adult education in Germany, 1800–1933. (Doctoral dissertation, University of California, 1966). *University Microfilms, Inc., 66–15,* 469.

Plomin, R. & De Fries, J. (2000). In Gottfredson, L., *The Scientific American book of the brain*. Connecticut: The Lyons Press.

Podeshi, R. L. (1987). Andragogy: Proofs or premises? *Lifelong learning: An omnibus of practice and research, 11* (N3), 14–16.

Pöggeler, F. (Ed.). (1975). The state and adult education: Historical and systematical aspects. Cited in H. Zdarzil (1990), *On the understanding of politics and adult educations since 1945*. Frank am Main, Germany: Verlag Peter Lang.

Pöggeler, F. (Ed.). (1990). *The state and adult education: Historical and systematical aspects*. Frank am Main, Germany: Verlag Peter Lang.

Pöggeler, F. (1992). Germany: Technical University of Aachen. P. Jarvis, *Perspectives on adult education and training in Europe*. The National Institute of Adult Continuing Education.

Pöggeler, F. (1996). Adult education as a democratic life style and a process of learning democracy. In J. Jug and F. Pöggeler (Ed.) *Democracy and adult education: Ideological changes and educational consequences*. Frank am Main, Germany: Verlag Peter Lang.

Pöggeler, F. (1998). History of adult education as history of adult educators: bio graphical aspects of Andragogical historiography. M. Friedenthal-Haase (Ed.), (1998) *Personality and biography: Proceedings of the sixth international conference on the history of adult education*. Frankfurt am Main, Germany: Verlag Peter Lang.

Pöggeler, F. (1999). *Introduction to andragogy*. (Oliver Walherr Trans.). Oklahoma: Tulsa (Original work published 1974).

Polturzycki, J. (1993). The Netherlands: *Rethinking adult education for development* (1st ed.). Ljubljana, Slovenia: Slovenia Ministry of Science and Technology.

Pratt, D. D. (1988). Andragogy as a relational construct. *Adult Education Quarterly, 38* (N3), 160–181.

Prokop, E. (1993). Germany. *Rethinking adult education for development*. 1st ed. Ljubljana, Slovenia: Slovenia Ministry of Science & Technology.

Rachal, J. R. (1994). *Andragogical and pedagogical methods compared: A review of the experimental literature.* University of Southern Mississippi.

Rachal, J. R. (2002). Andragogy's Detectives: A critique of the present and a proposal for the future. *Adult Education Quarterly, 52* (N3), 210–225.

Reischmann, J. (1993). Germany. *Rethinking adult education for development.* 1st ed. Ljubljana, Slovenia: Slovenia Ministry of Science & Technology.

Reischmann, J. Bron, M., & Jelenc, Z. (1999). Comparative adult education 1998. The contribution of ISCAE to an emerging field of study. Paper, Slovenian Institute for Adult Education, Ljubljana; International Society for Comparative Adult Education, Bamberg (Germany).

Reischmann, J. (2004). Andragogy. History, Meaning, Context, Function. http// web.unibamberg.de/ppp/andragogik/Andragogy/index.htm

Restak, R. M. (2000). *Mysteries of the mind.* Washington, D.C.: National Geographic.

Restak, R. M. (2001). *The secret life of the brain.* New York: Dana Press and Joseph Henry Press.

Röhrig, P. (1990). The relation between workers' education and state in Germany. Pöggeler (Ed.), *The state and adult education: Historical and systematical aspects.* Frankfurt am Main, Germany: Verlag Peter Lang.

Rothstein, J. M. (2000). Neuroscience and spinal cord injury: Plasticity in the brain, in the spinal cord and in our way of thinking. *American Physical Therapy Association, 80* (N7), 650–652.

Rowe, J. W., & Kahn, R. L. (1997). Successful aging. *The Gerontologist, 37* (N4), 433–440.

Russell, B. (1972). *A history of western philosophy.* New York: Simon and Schuster.

Russell, P. (1979). *The Brain Book.* New York: Penguin Group.

Rybash, J. M., Roodin, P. A., & Santrock, J. W. (1991). *Adult development and aging* (2nd ed.). William C. Brown.

Salthouse, T. A. (1982). *Adult cognition: An experimental psychology of human aging.* New York: Springer-Verlag.

Salthouse, T. A. (1985). *A theory of cognitive aging.* Amsterdam: North Holland.

Salthouse, T. A. (1991). *Theoretical perspectives on cognitive aging.* Hillsdale, NJ: Lawrence Erlbaum.

Sandmann, L. R. (1997). Adult learning—a joy, a tool, a right and a shared responsibility. *Adult Learning, 9* (N2), 5–6.

Santook, J. W. (1985). *Adult development and aging.* Dubuque, IA: William C. Brown.

Savicevic, D. M. (1981). Adult education systems in European socialist coun tries: Similarities and differences. W. S. Griffith and H. U. McClusky (Ed.), *Comparing Adult Education Worldwide.* San Francisco: Jossey-Bass.

Savicevic, D. M. (1989). Conceptions of andragogy in different countries: Com parative consideration. University of Belgrade, Yugoslavia. (Unpublished paper)

Savicevic, D. M. (1990). Contemporary trends in adult education research in Yugoslavia. *International Journal of Lifelong Education, 9* (N2), 129–135.

Savicevic, D. M. (1991). Modern conceptions of andragogy: a European frame work. *Studies in the Educations of Adults, 23* (N2), 179–201.

Savicevic, D. M. (1995). Understanding andragogy in Europe and America: comparing and contrasting. Paper presented at the international conference on research in comparative andragogy, Bamberg, Germany. (Unpublished manuscript)

Savicevic, D. M. (1996). Universities and adult education in the Federal Repub lic of Yugoslavia. *International Journal of University Adult Education, 35* (N2), 89–101.

Sax, G. (1979). *Foundations of educational research.* Englewood Cliffs, NJ: Pren tice Hall.

Schaie, K. W., & Willis, S. L. (1986). Can decline in adult intellectual function ing be reversed? *Developmental Psychology, 22* (N2), 223–232.

Scherer, M. (1997). *How do children learn?* Association for Supervision and Cur riculum Development.

Schmelzer, G. (Ed.). (1978). *Adult education in the German Democratic Republic.* European Centre for Leisure and Education.

Schulz, R., & Salthouse, T. (1999). *Adult development and aging myths and emerging realities.* New Jersey: Prentice Hall, Saddle River.

Sheridan, J. (1989). Rethinking andragogy: The case for collaborative learning in continuing higher education. *Continuing Higher Education,* 2–6.

Sherman, R. R., & Webb, R. B. (1988). *Qualitative research in education: Focus and methods.* London: The Falmer Press.

Simpson, J. A. (1964). Andragogy. *Adult education, England.*

Sims, B. B. (1968). *Immortals of philosophy and religion Confucius.* New York: Franklin Watts.

Sinnott, J. D. (Ed.). (1994). *Interdisciplinary handbook of adult lifespan learning.* Westport, CT: Greenwood Press.

Smith, M. K. (1998). Andragogy. *The informal education home page.* http://www.infed.or/biblio/b-anda.htm.

Smith, M. K. (1999). *Social pedagogy.* The informal education homepage http://www.infed.org/biblio/b-socped.htm.

Smith, R. M. (1993). America. *Rethinking adult education for development.* 1st ed. Ljubljana, Slovenia: Slovenia Ministry of Science & Technology.

Solomon, E. P., Berg, L. R., & Martin, D. W. (1999). *Biology.* Fort Worth, Texas: Saunders College.

Sopher, M. J. (2003). An historical biography of Malcolm S. Knowles: The remaking of an adult educator, University of Wisconsin-Madison, Department of Continuing, Adult and Vocational Education. Unpublished Doctor of Philosophy Dissertation.

Sousa, D. (1998). Is the fuss about brain research justified? *Education Week* (Vol. XVIII) No. 16, pp. 35, 52. Bethesda, MD.

Sprenger, M. (1999). *Learning and memory: The brain in action.* Alexandra: Association for Supervision and Curriculum Development.

Stewart, D. W. (1987). *Adult learning in America: Eduard Lindeman and his agenda for lifelong education.* Malabar, FL: Robert E. Krieger.

Stuart, M., & Hake, B. J. (Eds.) (1994). *Cultural and intercultural experiences in European adult education.* Leeds University, England.

Stubblefield, H. W. (1990). The state and adult education in the U.S.A. Franz Pöggeler (Ed.) *The state and adult education: Historical and systematical aspects.* Frankfurt am Main, Germany: Verlog Peter Lang.

Stubblefield, H. W. (1993). America. *Rethinking adult education for development.* 1st ed. Ljubljana, Slovenia: Slovenia Ministry of Science & Technology.

Studies in the education of adults. England: National institute of Adult Continuing Education (1987).

Susan, I. (1989). Teaching adults: Is it different? Eric Clearinghouse Adult, Career, and Vocational Education, Columbus, Ohio. EDO-CE-89-82 R188062005.

Svetina, M. (1994). *Rethinking adult education for development II.* Conference Proceedings, Slovene Adult Education Centre, Ljubljana, Slovenia.

Sylvester, R. (1994). How emotions affect learning. *Educational Leadership, 52* (N2), 106–111.

Sylvester, R. (1995). *A celebration of neurons.* Alexandria, Virginia: Association of Supervision and Curriculum Development.

Sylvester, R. (1998). *An interview with Robert Sylvester.*

Tanapat, P., Hastings, N. B., & Gould, E. (2001). 'Adult neurogenesis in the hippocampal formation.' Department of Psychology, Princeton University, Princeton, New Jersey.

Taylor, E., & Kaye, T. (1986). Andragogy by design? Control and self-direction in the design of an open university course. *Helping Adults Learn at a Distance, 23* (NI), 62–69.

Tennant, M. (1995). *Learning and change in the adult years: A developmental perspective.* San Francisco, Jossey-Bass.

Tennant, M., & Pogson, P. (1995). *Learning and change in the adult years.* San Francisco: Jossey-Bass.

Terry, E. F. (1988). Using andragogy to foster moral development of adults within the institutional church. *Lifelong Learning: An Omnibus of Practice and Research, 12* (N2), 4–6.

Teyler, T. (1978). *Brain and learning.* Stanford: Greylock.

The International Society of Comparative Study (1999). No. 19, Summer 1999. Bamberg, Germany.

Thompson, G. (1989). The complete adult educator: A reconceptualization of andragogy and pedagogy. *Canadian Journal of University Continuing Education, 15* (N1), 1–13.

Thompson, R. F. (1985*). The brain: An introduction to neuroscience.* New York, W. H. Freeman and Company.

Thorndike, E. L., Bregman, E. O., Cobb, M. V. and Woodyard, E. (1926). *The measurement of intelligence.* New York: Teachers College, Columbia University.

Thurstone, L. L. (1960). *The nature of intelligence.* Paterson: Littlefield, Adams and Company.

Tice, E. (1997). Educating adults: A matter of balance. *Adult Learning, 9* (NI), 18–21.

Titmus, C. J. (1989a). Adult education research: Western Europe. Colin J. Titmus (Ed.), *Lifelong Education for Adults*. University of Leeds, U.K.: Pergamon Press.

Titmus, C. J. (1989b). Lifelong education for adults: An international handbook. University of Leeds, U.K.: Pergamon Press.

Titmus, C. J., Buttedahl, P., Ironside, D., & Lengrand, P. (Eds.). (1979). *Terminology of adult education*. For the International Bureau of Education, UNESCO.

Traub, J. (1998). *Multiple intelligence disorder*. The new republic. New York: Lippincott.

Tuijnman, A. C. (Ed.). (1996). *International encyclopedia of adult education and training*. Paris, France: Pergamon Press.

Tulving, E., & Craik, F. I. M. (2000). *The Oxford handbook of memory*. New York: Oxford University Press.

Turkinton, C. (1996). The brain encyclopedia. Checkmark Books.

Tymowski, J. (1993). *The Netherlands: Rethinking adult education for development* (1st ed.). Ljubljana, Slovenia: Slovenia Ministry of Science and Technology.

Ulich, M. E. (1965). *Patterns of adult education*. New York: Pageant Press.

Usher, R., & Bryant, I. (1989). *Adult education as theory, practice, and research*. London: Routledge.

Van Dalen, D. B. (1973). *Understanding educational research*. 3rd ed. New York: McGraw-Hill.

Van Gent, B. (1989) 'Andragogy and andragology in the Netherlands: Issues in the definition of a scientific discipline", *Nottingham studies in the theory and practice of the education of adults*. Hake & Morgan (Eds.). Department of Adult Education, University of Nottingham.

Van Gent, B. (1991). *Basisboek andragologie*, Boom Meppel, Amsterdam.

Van Gent, B. (1996). Andragogy. Albert C. Tuijnman (Ed.)., *International encyclopedia of adult education and training*. Oxford: Pergamon Press.

Van Gent, B. (1998). *Tonko Ten Have—1906–1975*. Personality and biography: *Proceedings of the sixth international conference on history of adult education*.

Van Gent, B., Notten, A. L. T., en van Stegeren, W. F. (Ed.). (1984). *Welzijn swerk en Wetenschap: Hoofdstukken uit. De andragologie. Samson Uitgeverij Alphen aan den Rijn/Brussel*. Translated by J. Hendrik Erenstein (2000). Florida: Palm Harbor.

Verbiet, E. (1984). *Andragogie: Dialoog En Verhaal*. Swets and Zeitlinger.

Vos Savant, M., & Fleischer, L. (1990). *Brain building*. New York: Banton Books.

Walker, R. (2002). *Encyclopedia of the human body*. New York, DK Publishing.

Warren, C. (1989). Andragogy and N. F. S. Grundtvig: A critical link. *Adult Education Quarterly, 39* (N4), 211–223.

Wechsler, D. (1944). *The measurement of adult intelligence*. Baltimore, Maryland: Williams and Wilkins.

Weinberg, J (1991). 'Training in the Federal Republic of Germany.' Peter Jarvis & Alan Chadwick's (Eds.) *Training adult educators in Western Europe*. Routledge.

Weingand, D. E. (Ed.). (1996). A reminder about andragogy. *A Journal of Education for Library and Information Science, 37* (N1), 160–167.

Welford, A. T. (1958). *Aging and human skill*. The Nuffield Foundation, Oxford University Press.

Whalley, L. (2001). *The aging brain*. New York: Columbia University Press.

Wiersma, W. (1995). *Research methods in education: An introduction*. Boston: Allyn & Bacon.

Wilson, C. A. (2003). *A Comparative Study of the Historical Development of Andragogy and the Formation of Its Scientific foundation: in Germany and the*

United States of America, 1833–1999. Unpublished doctoral dissertation, Oral Roberts University, Tulsa, OK.

Wilson, I. (2000). *Jesus the evidence.* Washington, DC: Regency.

Woodruff-Pak, D. S. (1988). *Psychology and Aging.* Englewood Cliffs: Prentice Hall.

Yeo, G. (1982). "Eldergogy" A specialized approach to education for elders. *Life long Learning,* 5 (N5), 4–7.

Yonge, G. D. (1985). Andragogy and pedagogy two ways. Adult Education Quarterly, 35 (N3), 160–167.

Zdarzil, H. (1990). *On the understanding of politics and adult educations since 1945.* Frankfurt am Main, Germany: Verlag Peter Lang.

Zmeyon, S. I. (1998). Andragogy: origins, developments, and trends. *International Review of Education,* 44 (N1), 103–108.

978-0-595-38766-3
0-595-38766-7

Made in the USA
San Bernardino, CA
29 March 2013